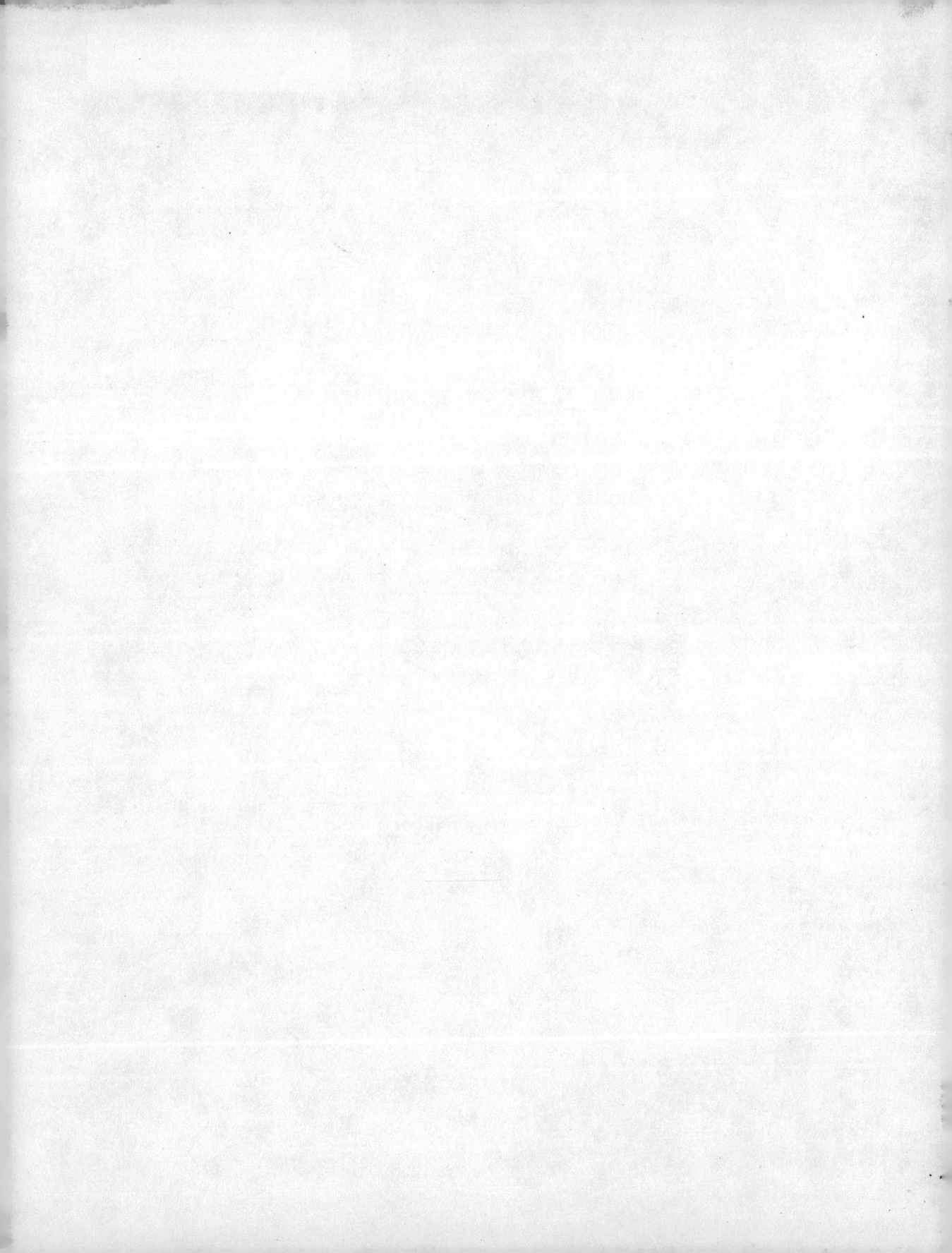

EXPLORING MUSIC 3

Eunice Boardman • Beth Landis

illustrated by Joe Smith

CALIFORNIA STATE SERIES
Published by
CALIFORNIA STATE DEPARTMENT OF EDUCATION
Sacramento, 1967

Consultants

Milton Babbitt	Harry Coopersmith	Kurt Miller
Bjornar Bergethon	Lucrecia R. Kasilag	Juan Orrego-Salas
Robert W. Buggert	Egon Kraus	Virginia Stroh Red
Chou Wen-chung	Alan Lomax	Henrietta Yurchenco

Acknowledgments

Grateful acknowledgment is given to the following authors and publishers:

The Boy Scouts Association of Great Britain for "We're All Together Again" from the *Boy Scout Song Book*.

The Consulado General de Costa Rica for the "Nonsense Song" from *Bailes Tipicos del Guanacaste*.

Dodd, Mead & Company for "Wishes." Reprinted by permission of Dodd, Mead & Company from *Dreamland Shores* by Norman Ault.

Doubleday & Company, Inc. for Opening Poem, "What Is Blue," "What Is White," "What Is Green," "What Is Red" from *Hailstones and Halibut Bones* by Mary O'Neill, Copyright © 1961 by Mary Gibbons O'Neill. Reprinted by permission of Doubleday & Company.

Doubleday & Company, Inc. for "What Is Black" by Mary O'Neill, copyright © 1960 by the Curtis Publishing Company, from *Hailstones and Halibut Bones* by Mary O'Neill. Reprinted by permission of Doubleday & Company.

Frederick Harris Music Company Limited for "'Twas in the Moon of Wintertime," words by J. E. Middleton, published by permission of the copyright owners, The Frederick Harris Music Company Limited, Oakville, Ontario.

Girl Scouts of the United States of America for "Navaho Happy Song" from the *Girl Scout Pocket Songbook*. Used by permission.

From *Cricket Songs*: Japanese Haiku, translated and © 1964, by Harry Behn. Reprinted by permission of Harcourt, Brace & World, Inc.

Harcourt, Brace & World, Inc. for "Hallowe'en" from *The Little Hill*, copyright, 1949, by Harry Behn. Reprinted by permission of Harcourt, Brace & World, Inc.

"Afternoon on a Hill" from *Collected Poems*, Harper & Row. Copyright 1917, 1945 by Edna St. Vincent Millay.

Holt, Rinehart and Winston, Inc. for "The Little Jesus Came to Town" from *The Selected Poems of Lizette Woodworth Reese*. Copyright 1926 by Holt, Rinehart and Winston, Inc. Copyright renewed 1954 by C. Reese Dietrich. Reprinted by permission of Holt, Rinehart and Winston, Inc.

Holt, Rinehart and Winston, Inc. for "A Little Song of Life" from *A Wayside Lute* by Lizette Woodworth Reese. All rights reserved. Reprinted by permission of Holt, Rinehart and Winston, Inc.

For "Hallowe'en," music by John Wood; for "Come Boating with Me," words by Lansing MacDowell; for "Hiking Song," words by Charles Winter; all from *Songtime 4* by Vera Russel, et al. Copyright © 1963 by Holt, Rinehart and Winston of Canada Limited, Publishers, Toronto.

Charles Scribner's Sons for "Christmas Eve." Reprinted with the permission of Charles Scribner's Sons from *The Open Door* by Marion Edey and Dorothy Grider. Copyright © 1949 Marion Edey and Dorothy Grider.

Waterloo Music Company Limited, Waterloo, Ontario, Canada for the words to "Land of the Silver Birch" from *Folk Songs of Canada* by Fowke-Johnston, 1954.

Music autography by Maxwell Weaner

Contents

Let's Explore Music

Have you ever gone exploring for hidden treasure? Did you have a map? Were there directions to guide you?

Your music book is a treasure map! It will help you find many wonderful treasures. The pages are filled with directions to help you as you explore. Be sure to follow them carefully.

Sometimes the map suggests that you sing as you explore. At other times the map hints that the best way to find the treasure is to dance or play an instrument. You may need to listen to a record in order to know which path to take.

There is one special thing about this treasure map. You will not have to wait until the end of the trail to find the prize. As you explore, you will be able to enjoy musical treasures all along the way.

There Are Many Flags in Many Lands

Composer Unknown
Words by M. H. Howliston

In march time

There are man-y flags in man-y lands,

There are flags of ev-ery hue;

But there is no flag, how-ev-er grand,

Like our own Red, White,— and — Blue.

Then hur - rah   for the   flag,   our   coun - try's   flag,

Its   stripes   and   white   stars,   too;

For there   is   no   flag   in   an - y   land

Like   our   own   Red,   White, __ and __   Blue.

For the Beauty of the Earth

Music by Conrad Kocher
Words by Folliott S. Pierpont

Read the words of this song and find the things for which we are thankful. The beautiful melody strengthens the thoughts expressed in the words.

1. For the beau-ty of the earth,
2. For the won-der of each hour
3. For the joy of hu-man love,

For the beau-ty of the skies,
Of the day and of the night,
Broth-er, sis-ter, par-ent, child,

For the love which from our birth
Hill and vale, and tree and flow'r,
Friends on earth, and friends a-bove,

O-ver and a-round us lies,
Sun and moon, and stars of light,
For all gen-tle thoughts and mild,

Lord of all, to thee we raise

This our hymn of grate-ful praise.

4

For Health and Strength

Traditional Round

For health and strength and dai - ly food,

We give thee thanks, O Lord.

Hiking Song

Scandinavian Song
Words by Charles Winter

There are many ways to explore music. One way is to sing the stanzas of a song differently when the words suggest different moods. How might you sing the first and second stanzas of this song?

1. The morn-ing is bright and we're gay, Fa - le - ra!
2. The night shad-ows slow-ly close in, Fa - le - ra!

We are hap-py to be out this love-ly day, Fa - le - ra!
We're so tired __ we don't know just where we've been, Fa - le - ra!

We stride a-long with ease, charm-ing birds out of the trees,
We stum-ble thro' the door; we are wea-ry and foot-sore,

As we sing the songs we please on our way, Fa - le - ra!
But we'll sing one cho-rus more com-ing in, Fa - le - ra!

Washington Post March

by John Philip Sousa

A **march** is one of the most cheerful and exciting kinds of
music. It makes us want to walk along beside a band with
our heads high.
Can you tell why?

In this march there are three tunes.
Can you hear all three?
Can you hear them repeated?

Listen for the mellow tone of the **clarinets** as they play
the third tune.
Listen for the rhythmic accompaniment beneath this tune in
the short, crisp tones of the low-voiced **French horns.**
Name some other instruments you hear in the march.

Musical compositions are often played by a **band** or an
orchestra. What makes a band sound different from an
orchestra? Which one plays this march?

John Philip Sousa is often called the American March King
because he composed so many marches which people like.
Your grandfather might have seen him directing a band.

The Story of Noah

Words and Music by
John Jacob Niles

With humor

1. Now did-n't old No-ah build an Ark?
2. Oh, an-i-mals come in two by two,

Built it out ___ of ___ hick-o-ry bark.
Rhi - noc - er - os and the kan - ga - roo.

Oh, an-i-mals come in one by one,
Oh, an-i-mals come in three by three,

Cow a - chew-in' on a car-a-way bun.
Bear a - hug-gin' on a bum-ble-y bee.

Refrain

Oh, who built the Ark? No-ah built it.

Who built the Ark? Old No-ah built it.

Who built the Ark? Old No - ah built it,

Cut - tin' his ___ tim - bers down. ___

3. Oh, animals come in four by four,
Two by the window and two by the door.
Oh, animals come in five by five,
Thus those animals did arrive.
Refrain

4. Oh, animals come in six by six,
Hyena laughin' at the monkey's tricks.
Oh, animals come in seven by seven,
Says the ant to the elephant, "Who is you shovin'?"
Refrain

5. Oh, animals come in eight by eight,
Noah shouted, "Boys, shut that gate!"
Oh, animals come in nine by nine,
Noah hollered, "Boys, cut the line!"
Refrain

Alouette

French-Canadian Folk Song

Our musical explorations take us all over the world. This song comes from our French-Canadian neighbors. Listen to the record to learn the French words.

Refrain

A - lou - et - te, gen - tille a - lou - et - te,

A - lou - et - te, je te plu - me - rai. *Fine*

Verse

1. Je te plu-me-rai la têt', je te plu-me-rai la têt',
2. Je te plu-me-rai le bec, je te plu-me-rai le bec,

D.C. al Fine

(1). Et la têt', et la têt', }
A - lou - ette, a - lou - ette, } Oh!

(2). Et le bec, et le bec, }
Et la têt', et la têt', } Oh!
A - lou - ette, a - lou - ette, }

3. Je te plumerai les pattes
4. Je te plumerai les ailes
5. Je te plumerai le dos
6. Je te plumerai la queue

10

This song is from Costa Rica, a country
which is south of the United States.
Can you find it on a map of the world?

Nonsense Song

Costa Rican Folk Song
Words Adapted by
Ruth De Cesare

With humor

1. I'll tell you a lit - tle sto - ry;
2. Now list - ten, this tale is bet - ter,

it's the best you will be hear - ing:
so be - lieve my tes - ti - mo - ny:

A chick - en jumped from a cook - ing pot
A rab - bit once hopped a ten - foot fence

and van - ished in a clear - ing!
and roped a run - ning po - ny!

3. These stories we tell are foolish,
   but it happened in a shower:
   A little plane circled in the rain
   and landed on a flower!

4. Now think of another story;
   it's the funny ones that please us.
   So just do your best, we'll sing the rest;
   then someone else can tease us!

11

Blow Ye Winds

Sea Chantey

A chantey is a sailor's song. This chantey was often sung by the sailors of early America as they prepared to set sail.

Heartily

1. They ad - ver - tise in Bos - ton town,
2. They send you to New Bed - ford fair,
3. They tell you of the clip - per ships,

New York, and Buf - fa - lo,
That fa - mous whal - ing port,
A - go - ing in and out,

Five hun - dred brave A - mer - i - cans
And give you to some stran - gers there
And say you'll take five hun - dred whale

A - whal - ing for to go, _____ sing - ing:
To board and fit you out; _____ sing - ing:
Be - fore you're six months out; _____ sing - ing:

12

Refrain

Blow ye winds of morn - ing,

And blow ye winds, heigh ho!

Clear a - way the run - ning gear,

And blow ye winds, heigh ho!

Explore different ways of adding movement as you sing this song.
Pretend that you are hauling in the anchor or raising the sail.
What other things might you do to prepare for sailing? Be sure
your movements match the movement of the music.

13

Sing to Begin the Day

"We're All Together Again" is a good song to begin your school day. Sing these songs, or choose others you enjoy.

We're All Together Again

British Scout Song

Vigorously

We're all to-geth-er a - gain, we're here, we're here! __

We're all to-geth-er a - gain, we're here, we're here! __

Who knows when we'll be all to - geth-er a - gain,

Sing-ing all to-geth-er a - gain: we're here, we're here! __

Some Folks Do

Words and Music by
Stephen Foster

Stephen Foster is one of our best-known
American composers. He wrote songs
that captured the spirit of American
life during the time of Abraham Lincoln.

Merrily

1. Some folks like to sigh,
2. Some folks fear to smile,
3. Some folks get gray hairs,

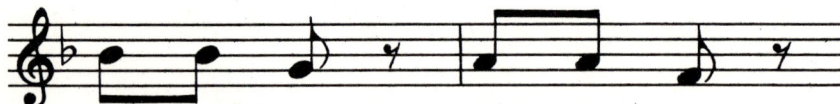

Some folks do, some folks do;

Some folks long to die,
Oth - ers laugh through guile,
Brood - ing o'er their cares,

16

But that's not me nor you.

Refrain

Long live the mer-ry, mer-ry heart That

laughs by night and day, Like the queen of

mirth, No mat-ter what some folks say.

A Little Song of Life

Music by William S. Haynie
Words by Lizette Woodworth Reese

Simply

1. Glad that I live am I, _____
2. Af - ter the sun the rain, _____
3. All that we need to do, _____

That the sky is blue, _____
Af-ter the rain the sun, _____
Be we low or high, _____

Glad for the coun - try lanes
This is the way ___ of life
Is ___ to see that we grow

And the fall of dew. ___
Till the work is done. ___
Ev - er near - er the sky. ___

Play the following melody pattern on the bells as an accompaniment.

B D C   C E D   B D C   D C B

18

Rondo for Bassoon and Orchestra
from *Andante and Rondo, Op. 35*
by Carl Maria von Weber

The **bassoon** is sometimes called the clown of the orchestra because of its special sound. It can play high and low in quick rhythms and do various musical tricks. The bassoon can also sing in a melodious voice.

Listen to the *Rondo for Bassoon and Orchestra*. The music seems to go round and round because the main theme or tune is played again and again. We hear the main theme and then a series of new themes. The main theme is repeated after each new theme.

The bassoon is the solo instrument and introduces each new theme. The orchestra sometimes imitates the bassoon. Sometimes it whispers a soft accompaniment while the bassoon plays the melody.

How many times does the bassoon play the main theme?

Can you hear the **oboe** imitating the bassoon by playing the main theme?

Can you hear the French horns introduce one of the bassoon melodies and then accompany it?

Can you hear the oboe weaving a little pattern with the bassoon?

How does the bassoon show off its tricks at the end?

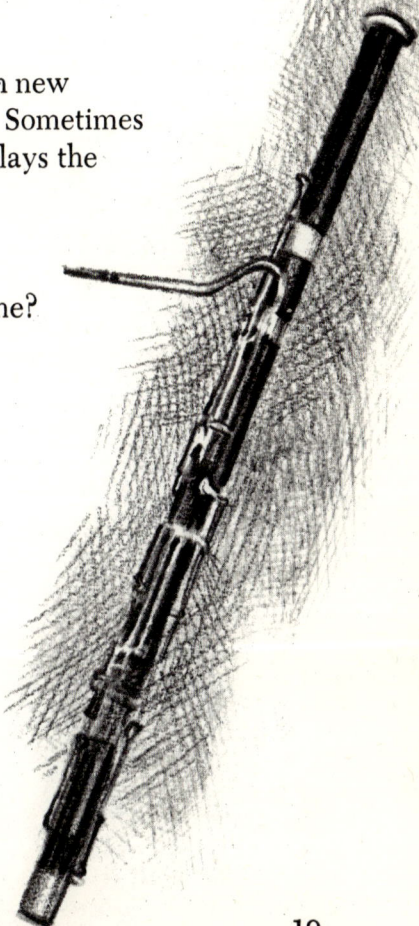

America, the Beautiful

Music by Samuel A. Ward
Words by Katharine Lee Bates

Majestically

1. O beau - ti - ful for spa - cious skies,
2. O beau - ti - ful for pa - triot dream

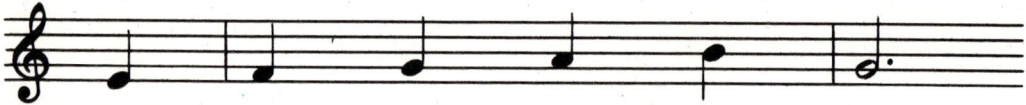

For am - ber waves of grain,
That sees, be - yond the years,

For pur - ple moun - tain maj - es - ties
Thine al - a - bas - ter cit - ies gleam,

A - bove the fruit - ed plain!
Un - dimmed by hu - man tears!

A - mer - i - ca! A - mer - i - ca!

God shed his grace on thee,

And crown thy good with broth - er - hood

From sea to shin - ing sea!

You Shall Reap

Spiritual

You shall reap ___ just what you sow, You shall

reap what you sow On the moun - tain, in the

val - ley, ___ You shall reap ___ just what you sow.

1. Broth-er,
2. Sis - ter, } you shall reap ___ just what you sow, You shall
3. Sin - ner,

reap what you sow On the moun - tain, in the

val - ley, ___ You shall reap ___ just what you sow.

Sur le Pont d'Avignon

French Folk Song

Refrain

Sur le Pont d'A - vi- gnon, L'on y dan - se, l'on y dan - se,

Sur le Pont d'A - vi - gnon, L'on y dan - se tout en rond.

Verse

1. Les mes - sieurs font comm' ci,
2. Les bell's dam's font comm' ci,   Et puis en - cor' comm' ça.
3. Les sol - dats font comm' ci,

Music Moves in Rhythm

We hear and feel the movement of music through its **rhythm.**

Listen to music and feel the **beat.**
The beat is the steady pulse of music.
Accents group the beats in twos or threes.
Accented beats are heavy; other beats are light:
    HEAVY light HEAVY light, or HEAVY light light HEAVY light light.
In a marching rhythm the accents group the beats in twos:
    LEFT right LEFT right LEFT right.
In a swinging rhythm the accents group the beats in threes:
    ONE two three ONE two three ONE two three ONE two three.

Listen to music and hear **patterns** of rhythm.
The patterns of rhythm are made of tones that move in relation
to the beat.
Patterns of rhythm may include tones that are
    the **same length** as the beat,
    longer than the beat,
    shorter than the beat.

beat: —— —— —— ——
same length: —— —— —— ——
longer: ———— ————
shorter: — — — — — — — —

Get on Board

Spiritual

With strong accent

Get on board, lit - tle chil - dren, Get on

board, lit - tle chil - dren, Get on board, lit - tle

chil - dren, There's room for man - y a more. *Fine*

The gos - pel train's a - com - ing, I hear it just at

hand; ___ I hear the car - wheels rum - bling and

D.C. al Fine

roll - ing through the land. So

This song moves in threes. Do songs which move in threes have a different feeling from those which move in twos? Give reasons for your answer.

Come Boating with Me

Italian Folk Song
Words by Lansing MacDowell

With flowing movement

Come boat - ing with me, _____

Come boat - ing with me, _____

Un - der the stars 'mid the sound of gui - tars,

Come boat - ing with me. _____

Play this accompaniment on the bells. Play on the **accented beats**.

Eb   C   Bb   G   Eb   C   Bb   G

C   Bb   Ab   G   Eb   C   Bb   G

Change the words of the third phrase and make new stanzas of your own.

27

Juchheidi, Juchheida

German Folk Song
Words Adapted

This hiking song from Germany has strong **accents.** Can you feel the accented beats as you sing and march around the room? Do the accents group the beats in **twos** or in **threes?**

With spirit

1. Hik - ing through the fields we go,
2. Through the woods we stroll a - long,

Juch - hei - di, juch - hei - da. E - ven in the
Lis - ten to our

ice and snow, Juch - hei - di, hei - da.
hap - py song,

In each sea - son of the year,
When the cuck - oo starts to sing,

Hik - ing brings us health and cheer.
We join in to greet the spring.

Refrain

Juch - hei - di, hei - di, hei - da, Juch - hei - di, juch - hei - da,

Juch - hei - di, hei - di, hei - da, Juch - hei - di, hei - da.

Turn the Glasses Over

American Singing Game

Music for dancing has strong rhythm. When you dance this song, move with the accent.

I've been to Haar - lem, I've been to Do - ver,

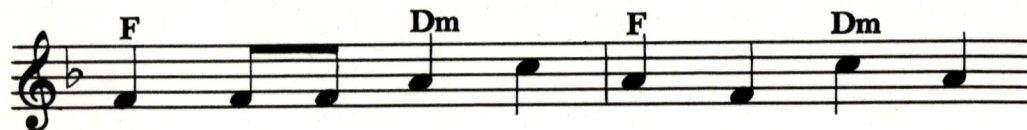

I've trav - eled this wide world all o - ver,

O - ver, o - ver, three times o - ver,

Drink what you have to drink and turn the glas - ses o - ver.

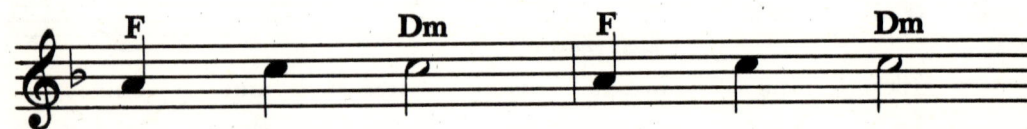

Sail - ing east, sail - ing west,

30

Sail - ing   o - ver   the   o - cean,

Bet - ter   watch   out   when the   boat be - gins   to   rock,

Or   you'll   lose   your   girl   in   the   o - cean.

Play this pattern on rhythm sticks as you sing.

O - ver,   o - ver, three times o - ver

You are playing on the **beat** which is the steady pulse.
In this song the beat is shown by a **quarter note:** ♩

The **rhythm patterns** in this song are made up of sounds of
different lengths.
As you sing, listen for tones that are held for two beats.
They are shown by **half notes:** ♩
Listen for tones that sound two to a beat.
They are shown by **eighth notes:** ♫

31

Sandy Land

American Singing Game
Words Adapted

Listen to the recording. Can you hear these percussion instruments in the accompaniment: blocks, cymbals, and xylophone?

1. Make my liv - ing in sand - y land,
2. Raise my ta - ters in sand - y land,
3. Keep on dig - ging in sand - y land,

Make my liv - ing in sand - y land,
Raise my ta - ters in sand - y land,
Keep on dig - ging in sand - y land,

Make my liv - ing in sand - y land,
Raise my ta - ters in sand - y land,
Keep on dig - ging in sand - y land,

La - dies, fare you well.

Plan an autoharp accompaniment.
The names of the chords you need to play are written above the staff. Be sure to play on the **accented beat.**

Old Sounds in Music

History tells us that man has always made music. The primitive people of America played drums to send signals and accompany dances. They sang to their children, and they sang at their work. Their voices, instruments, and dances were used in prayers, ceremonies, and recreation. They sang chant melodies with only a few tones. They played intricate rhythms as well as simple ones.

In the Southwest we can still see and hear the dances and music of the Navaho Indians. Listen to the "Corn Grinding Song" and the "Silversmith Song" on your record.

Canoe Song

American Indian Song

My pad - dle's keen and bright, Flash-ing with sil - ver.

Fol - low the wild goose flight, Dip, dip, and swing.

Navaho Happy Song

Navaho Indian Song

Hi yo hi yo ip si ni yah,

Hi yo hi yo ip si ni ___ yah,

Hi ___ yo hi yo ip si ni yah,

Repeat twice

Hi ___ yo hi yo ip si ni yah,

Ip si ni *Yah!*

Indians usually accompany their songs with a steady drum beat.
Add drum accompaniments to the Indian songs you have learned.

Play the drum and gourd rattles in rhythms of your own as the
Indians might have played when sending signals or accompanying
a dance.

Let someone dance as you play. Try different dance steps.
Choose the ones you like best.

Land of the Silver Birch

Canadian Folk Song

1. Land of the sil - ver birch, home of the bea - ver,
2. Down in the for - est, deep in the low - lands,
3. High on a rock - y ledge, I'll build a wig - wam,

Where still the might - y moose wan - ders at will,
My heart cries out for thee, hills of the north.
Close by the wa - ter's edge, si - lent and still.

Refrain

Blue lake and rock - y shore, I will re - turn once more.

Boom de de boom boom, Boom de de boom boom,

Boom de de boom boom, Boom ___ boom boom. ___

La cloche

Listen to the record to learn to pronounce the French words.

French Round

Din, don, din, don, C'est la clo-che du ma-tin,

Qui sonne au le-ver du jour: Bon-jour, bon-jour!

Listen as you sing this song.
The **accents** group the beats in twos.
Notice that the **bar lines** also group the beats in twos.
These groups are called **measures.**

Look at the numbers at the beginning of the song.
The upper number tells how the beats are grouped.
The lower number tells us what kind of note moves with the beat.
These numbers are called the **meter signature.**

In this song the meter signature is $\frac{2}{4}$.

It tells us that the song moves in twos and that the quarter note (♩) moves with the beat.

Sandy McNab

Traditional Round

1. There was an old fel - low named Sand - y Mc - Nab,

2. Who had for his sup - per a ver - y fine crab,

3. And had to be car - ried home in a cab.

Listen as you sing this song.
Do the accents group the beats in twos or in threes?

Look at the music.
Do the measures group the beats in twos or in threes?

Look at the numbers at the beginning of the song.
Does the upper number tell you that this song moves in twos or in threes?
Look at the lower number.
What kind of note will move with the beat?

Tinga Layo

Calypso Song from
the West Indies

Not too fast

Tin - ga Lay - o!   Come, lit - tle don - key, come;

Tin - ga Lay - o!   Come, lit - tle don - key, come.

1. My don - key   walk,   my don - key   talk,
2. My don - key   eat,   my don - key   sleep,

My don - key   eat with   a   knife   and   fork.
My don - key   kick with   his   two   hind   feet.

Tin - ga Lay - o! Come, lit - tle don - key, come;

Tin - ga Lay - o! Come, lit - tle don - key, come.

Listen to the record and hear this interesting rhythm pattern.

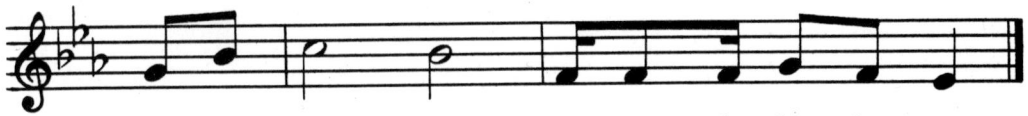

How many times does it appear in the song?
Listen for interesting patterns in the accompaniment.
Perhaps you can play one of them on rhythm sticks or claves.
Claves are short, thick sticks. The people in the West Indies
often use them to accompany their songs.

My Farm

Mi chacra

Argentine Folk Song
English Words Adapted

Briskly

Come, let us see my farm, for it is beau-ti-ful,
Ven - gan a ver mi cha - cra que es her - mo - sa,

Come, let us see my farm, for it is beau-ti-ful.
Ven - gan a ver mi cha - cra que es her - mo - sa.

1. El po - lli - to goes like this: } pi - pi ri,
1. *El po - lli - to ha - ce a sí:* } *pi - pi ri,*

El po - lli - to goes like this: } pi - pi ri.
El po - lli - to ha - ce a sí: } *pi - pi ri.*

Oh, come now my friend, Oh, come now my friend, Oh,
O ven, ca - ma - ra - da, ven, ca - ma - ra - da,

40

come a - long with me,   Oh,   come now my friend, Oh,
ven, O ven, O ven,   O   ven, ca - ma - ra - da,

come now my friend, Oh,   come a - long with me.
ven, ca - ma - ra - da,   ven, O ven, O ven.

el pollito

el patito

el chanchito

el gatito

el perrito

el burrito

2. *El patito* goes like this: *cuac, cuac*
3. *El chanchito* goes like this: *joinc, joinc*
4. *El gatito* goes like this: *miau, miau*
5. *El perrito* goes like this: *guau, guau*
6. *El burrito* goes like this: *iji, iji*

The Needle's Eye

American Singing Game

Liltingly

Oh, the nee - dle's eye that doth sup - ply The

thread that runs so tru - ly, There is
(There is

man - y a lass that I let pass,)
man - y a beau that I let go,)

Be - cause I want - ed you, _____

Be - cause I want - ed you, _____

Be - cause I want - ed you. _____

42

There's man - y a lass that I let pass,
(There's man - y a beau that I let go,)

Be - cause I want - ed you, _____

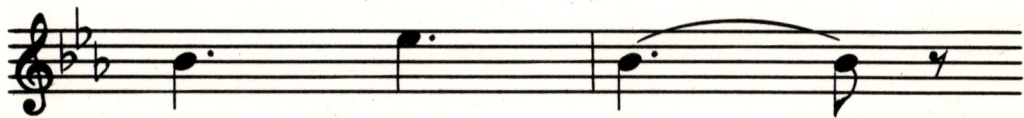

You, you, you, _____

Be - cause I want - ed you. _____

You will enjoy playing this singing game.
Join hands in a circle.
Choose one couple to form a "needle's eye" by joining right hands
in an arch.

To play the game, the circle moves to the left under the arch in
time to the music.
On the words "Because I wanted you," the couple forming the arch
catches someone in the circle.
This player then makes a new arch with the partner who stood
inside the circle.
The old partner goes to the center of the ring.

Hawaiian Boat Song

Hawaiian Folk Song
Words Adapted

The dreamy mood of this song fits
the romantic island life of Hawaii.

In my ca - noe I'm glid - ing, glid - ing;

My oars are flash - ing in the sun - light.

In my ca - noe I'm glid - ing, glid - ing;

The waves so gent - ly help me on.

Refrain

The u - ku - le - les, the u - ku - le - les,

My friends are strum - ming as we glide.__ glide.

You will enjoy playing the Hawaiian stick game with this song. Tap the floor with your sticks or tap them together or tap your partner's sticks. Play in rhythm with the song. Think of other ways you can play your sticks. Use one idea for the first two lines, another for the next two. You can use two ideas with the refrain.

Sing this song while someone plays the autoharp and a few children play the stick game.

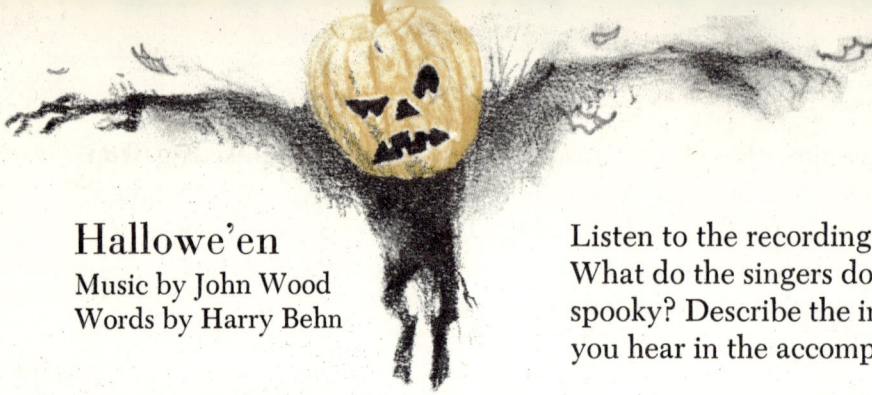

Hallowe'en

Music by John Wood
Words by Harry Behn

Listen to the recording of this song. What do the singers do to make it sound spooky? Describe the instruments that you hear in the accompaniment.

Mysteriously

1. To - night is the night when dead leaves fly
2. To - night is the night when leaves do sound
3. To - night is the night when pump - kins stare

Like witch - es on switch - es a - cross the sky,
Like gnomes in their homes far be - neath the ground,
Through brown sheaves and leaves al - most ev - ery - where,

When elf and sprite flit through the night,
When spooks and trolls creep out of holes
When ghoul and ghost and gob - lin host

On a moon - y sheen, on a moon - y sheen.
Dark and moss - y green, dark and moss - y green.
Dance a - round their queen, for it's Hal - low - e'en!

You can make up your own spooky accompaniment for this song.
List the words you think about at Halloween.
Chant them softly while part of the class sings, or play the rhythm pattern of the words on percussion instruments.

Enjoy the rhythm of this song as you
dance. In the third stanza, the boat
is so full it will hardly move. Show
this in your singing and dancing.

Four in a Boat

Appalachian Mountain Song

1. Four in a boat and the tide rolls high,
2. Choose your ___ part - ner and stay all day,
3. Eight in a boat and it won't go round,

Four in a boat and the tide rolls high,
Choose your ___ part - ner and stay all day,
Eight in a boat and it won't go round,

Four in a boat and the tide rolls high,
Choose your ___ part - ner and stay all day,
Eight in a boat and it won't go round,

Wait - ing for a pret - ty one to come by'm by.
We ___ don't ___ care ___ what the old folks say.
Swing ___ that ___ pret - ty one that you've just found.

47

Dance Your Own Dance

Every child is a special person.
He has a face of his own.
He has a mind of his own.
And he can hear music in his own way.

Try dancing your own dance with music.
Your dance may follow the rhythm or the melody
of the music.
It may follow the design of the music, or it may
follow the different instruments.
Think about the music all the time you are
dancing.
Let yourself be free to go with the music.

Dance of the Comedians
from *The Bartered Bride*

by Bedrich Smetana

"Dance of the Comedians" is music written for a scene in an opera, *The Bartered Bride*. It is the scene of a village festival. The "comedians" are dressed like circus performers. The village folk gather to watch the show.

Make a list of performers you have seen in the circus or at the fair. Listen to the music all the way through. What kinds of performers do you hear in this show?

As you listen again to the different sections of the music, try to imagine the various acts. How many acts do you think there are? Take turns dancing different acts and find good dances for each section.

Build a grand **finale** for your show in which all the groups repeat their dances with the exciting ending of Smetana's music. When you have practiced each act, make a continuous show by dancing the acts one after another. Finish with your grand finale.

49

Symphony No. 94 ("Surprise")
Third Movement

by Joseph Haydn

This is rollicking dance music played by an orchestra. Listen
to the music and hear Theme One. It has two parts which we
may call the "question" and "answer." Theme Two is a brisk
running tune with eight accents. Notice how many times Theme
One and Theme Two are repeated in the first section of the
composition. Listen to Theme Three in the middle section.
You will hear Theme One and Theme Two again in the last
section of the music.

Making up a class dance will help you know the music. Let
the class form a large circle and count off: question,
answer, question, answer. Find dance patterns you like for
each part of Theme One. Then take turns dancing the two parts
of the theme. Repeat the dance patterns each time you hear
the question and answer melodies.

Theme Two might be danced by a few children in the center of
the circle. Can you show the running tune and the accents
in your movements?

One child might dance the curly Theme Three. If he goes in
different directions with the different phrases, his dance
will look like the music sounds.

When you have discovered dance patterns you like for each of
the melodies, dance them with the music in one merry dance.

German Dance ("Sleighride")

by Wolfgang Amadeus Mozart

Mozart wrote many German dances which were used for ballroom dancing in his time. He lived in Austria at the same time that George Washington lived in our country. Look at the pictures of people of that time and decide what the style of this dance should be.

Listen to the music and discover the different tunes.
Call each tune by a different letter name.
Which tune gives this dance its nickname?

The class may plan a dance with the music.

Music Speaks in Melody

Listen to a beautiful **melody** and hear it soar and swell and
come to rest.
Melody speaks in **phrases** which are musical thoughts.
Melody moves with **rhythm.**

The melody of a song strengthens the meaning of the words.
It helps make the mood peaceful or humorous or merry.

We can sing melodies or play them on musical instruments.
We hear melodies in the music of orchestras and other
musical groups.

We enjoy the rise and fall of a melody as the tones move
high and **low.**
Tones of a melody move **up** and **down** because they have **pitch.**

Listen to music and hear **melody patterns.**
Patterns of melody are heard again and again.

Austrian Counting Song

Austrian Folk Song
Traditional Words

Easily

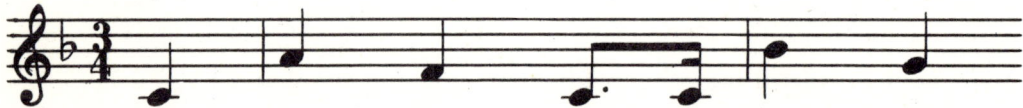

1. I count - ed in the heav - en,
2. White sheep grazed in the mead - ow,

where the moon __ shed its light;
ev - ery one __ wore a bell;

White stars that num - bered sev - en,
Each one fol - lowed its shad - ow

they were twin - kling so bright.
o'er the grass __ where it fell.

Refrain

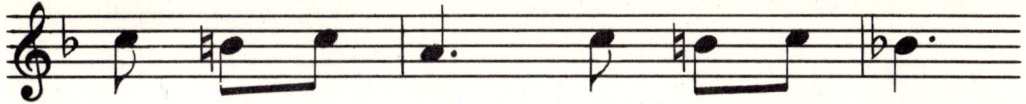

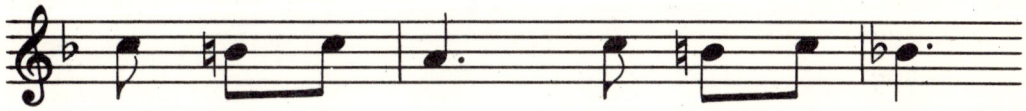

I count - ed one, I count - ed two,
I count - ed three, I count - ed four,
I count - ed five, I count - ed six,
I count - ed sev - en, good night!

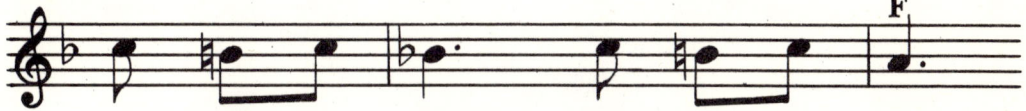

Play the bells as you count the stars. Use these three bells:

Decide which bell you will play for each star.

Ship A-Sailing

English Folk Song

Liltingly

1. I saw a ship___ a - sail - ing,
2. The four and twen - ty sail - ors,

A - sail - ing on the sea, _____
That stood be - tween the decks, _____

And it was deep - ly lad - en
Were four and twen - ty white mice

With pret - ty things for me. _____
With rings a - bout their necks. _____

There was can - dy in the cab - in
The ___ cap - tain was a duck, a duck

And ap - ples in the hold; ___
With a jack - et on his back; ___

The sails were made of sat - in
And when this fair - y ship set sail,

And the masts were made of gold. ___
The ___ cap - tain said, "Quack quack." ___

Compare this melody with the melody of the song "Clouds"
on the next page.
This melody has many large skips.
It covers a wide range of tones.
How is the mood of this song different from that of "Clouds"?

Clouds

Music by Arthur Frackenpohl
Words by Christina Rossetti

Listen to the recording of this song.
Describe the mood of the song. How does
the melody help you feel this mood? How
does the melody strengthen the words?

Wistfully

White sheep, white sheep, on a — blue — hill,

White sheep, white sheep, on a — blue — hill,

When the wind stops You all — stand still.

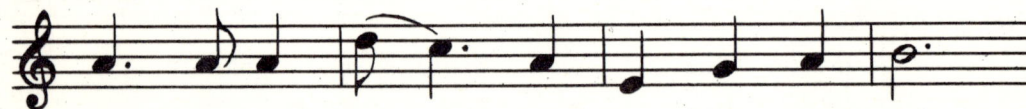

When the wind blows — You walk a - way slow.

White sheep, white sheep, Where do — you go? —

Suite No. 3 in D Major

Air

by Johann Sebastian Bach

The "Air" by Bach is one of his most loved melodies. Air is another word for melody or tune.

The violins begin the "Air" with a high tone which captures our attention like a bright star. Then the melody continues on its peaceful way and flows smoothly from tone to tone.

Underneath the melody we feel the steady pulse of the cellos and double basses. Other violins and violas weave soft melodies between the main theme and bass accompaniment.

The "Air" soars and swells and comes to rest, carrying us along in moods of quiet joy and pleasure.

Awake and Sing

Old German Hymn
Words Translated by
Catherine Winkworth

Joyously

Heav - en and ___ earth and sea and air,

All ___ their Mak - er's praise de - clare;

Wake, my ___ soul, a - wake and sing:

Now thy grate - ful prais - es bring.

The tones of a melody are represented by **notes** on the **staff.**
The notes move **up** and **down** by **steps** and **skips** on the **lines** and **spaces.**
Some songs move mostly by **steps** of the **scale.**

Play the melody of the first phrase of "Awake and Sing" on the bells.
It is based on the D **major** scale:

D	E	F♯	G	A	B	C♯	D	D	C♯	B	A	G	F♯	E	D
1	2	3	4	5	6	7	8	8	7	6	5	4	3	2	1

Play the first phrase of "Awake and Sing" beginning on C.
Here is the C **major** scale:

C	D	E	F	G	A	B	C	C	B	A	G	F	E	D	C
1	2	3	4	5	6	7	8	8	7	6	5	4	3	2	1

Harvest Song

Danish Song
Traditional Words

1. Out in the mead-ows the grain has been cra-dled,
2. Soon we shall har-vest the corn which is ri-pened;

Rye and wheat are stacked and soon the hay is in the barn.
Let us count our bless-ings as the grain is gath-ered in.

Trees have been shak-en and fruit has been gath-ered,
So in the full-ness of boun-ti-ful har-vest,

Home-ward now we wend our way up-on the fi-nal load.
Let us keep an o-pen heart for those who are in need.

Refrain

Glad-ness on ev-ery hand, Games and dance through-out the land;

Sing-ing mer-ri-ly we bind the hap-py har-vest wreath.

Some melodies move mostly by skips.
Play the first phrase of "Harvest Song" on the bells.
It is made up of these scale tones.

C	G	E	C
8	5	3	1

Play the first phrase of this song starting on D.

D	A	F♯	D
8	5	3	1

Melody patterns using these tones are often found in songs.

This Is My Father's World

Traditional English Melody
Adapted by Franklin L. Sheppard
Words by Maltbie D. Babcock

In the Bach "Air" you heard the sounds of many string instruments. Listen to the recording of this song and hear the sounds of a few string instruments.

1. This _ is my Fa - ther's world;
2. This _ is my Fa - ther's world;

And _ to my lis - t'ning ears,
The _ birds their car - ols raise.

All na - ture sings, and _ round me rings
The morn - ing light, the _ lil - y white,

The mu - sic of the _ spheres.
De - clare _ their Mak - er's _ praise.

This is my Fa - ther's world;
This is my Fa - ther's world;

I __ rest me in the thought
He __ shines in all that's fair;

Of rocks and trees, of __ skies and seas;
In the rus - tling grass I __ hear him pass;

His hands __ the won - ders __ wrought.
He speaks __ to me ev - ery - where.

The melody of this song is bright and strong like the words of the poem. It is a good song to sing all through the year. Sing it for your Thanksgiving program. "Harvest Song" and "For the Beauty of the Earth" are also good songs of thanksgiving.

Thanksgiving is an important American holiday. Many people celebrate harvest festivals, although the United States and Canada are the only nations that have national holidays set aside for giving thanks.

Oh, Go to Sleep, Nene

Philippine Folk Song
Words Adapted

Listen to the recording of this song.
The beautiful, rippling sounds which
you hear in the accompaniment are made
by the **harp.**

Tenderly

Oh, go to sleep, Ne - ne; _____

The time to sleep is nigh. _____

The sky is calm a - bove; _____

The sil - ver moon is bright. _____

Oh, go to sleep, Ne - ne; _____

The night will not be long. _____

Oh, sleep, Ne - ne, so sweet - ly,

And dream on wings of song. _____

Deaf Woman's Courtship

American Folk Song

The melody of this song is made up almost entirely of these tones.

D	A	F♯	D
8	5	3	1

Find a **melody pattern** in the song using three of the tones, using two of them, using only one. Can you sing the melody patterns with numbers? Can you play the patterns on the bells?

With humor

1. Old wom- an, old wom- an, Are you fond of card - ing?
2. Old wom- an, old wom- an, Are you fond of spin - ning?

Old wom - an, old wom- an, Are you fond of card - ing?
Old wom - an, old wom- an, Are you fond of spin - ning?

Speak a lit - tle loud - er, sir! I'm ver - y hard of hear - ing.
Speak a lit - tle loud - er, sir! I'm ver - y hard of hear - ing.

3. Old woman, old woman, Will you darn my stocking? *(2 times)*
Speak a little louder, sir! I'm very hard of hearing.

4. Old woman, old woman, Will you let me court you? *(2 times)*
Speak a little louder, sir! I just begin to hear you.

5. Old woman, old woman, Don't you want to marry me? *(2 times)*
Oh, my goodness gracious me! I think that now I hear you!

Ah, Poor Bird

Old English Melody
Words Adapted

Plaintively

Ah, poor bird, you are sad; but
Ah, poor bird, fly a - way; and

when you lived in yon - der wood your song was glad.
from the tree - top you can sing your song so gay.

Play this pattern on the bells as you sing.

D	E	F	F	G	A
1	2	3	3	4	5

This pattern is part of the D **minor** scale.
It helps us feel a different mood as we sing or listen to this song.
Compare the mood of "Ah, Poor Bird" with the mood of "Awake and Sing."

Two Waltzes

Frederic Chopin is known as the poet of the piano, and these waltzes are two of his best-known pieces. If you study the piano, you may someday play them.

Enjoy the waltzes many times during the year by listening to the record.
Listen for the swing of the waltz rhythm as it moves in threes.
Listen for the rippling melodies.
Listen for these melodies as they are repeated.
Listen for the major sound of one waltz and the minor sound of the other.

Waltz in D Flat Major ("Minute Waltz")

by Frederic Chopin

The "Waltz in D Flat Major" is nicknamed the "Minute Waltz."
Can you guess why?
In the second section of this waltz, the main tune begins
with these notes:

Can you learn to hum or whistle this tune with the record?

Waltz in C Sharp Minor

by Frederic Chopin

In the "Waltz in C Sharp Minor," Chopin wrote a page of music
which he said he liked better than any other page in all
his music. Listen for his favorite theme in the second
section of the waltz. The theme begins with these measures:

Try to hear and see the music at the same time. What do
you notice about the notes? Why do you suppose Chopin
liked this theme so much?

The Frog and the Mouse

American Folk Song

This song is based on the **D minor** scale.
Play the minor scale on the bells.

D E F G A Bb C D
1 2 3 4 5 6 7 8

1. There was a frog lived in a well,
2. He rode till he came to Mou - se's Hall,

Whip - see did - dle dee dan - dy O!

There was a mouse lived in a mill.
Where he most ten - der - ly did call,

Whip - see did - dle dee dan - dy O!

This frog he would a - woo - ing ride
"O Mis - tress Mouse, are you at home?

With sword and pis - tol by his side. }
And if you are, oh, please come down." }

With a har - um scar - um did - dle dum dar - um,

Whip - see did - dle dee dan - dy O!

3. "My Uncle Rat is not at home,"
Whipsee diddle dee dandy O!
"I dare not for my life come down."
Whipsee diddle dee dandy O!
Then Uncle Rat he soon comes home,
"And who's been here since I've been gone?"
With a harum scarum diddle dum darum,
Whipsee diddle dee dandy O!

4. "Here's been a fine young gentleman,"
Whipsee diddle dee dandy O!
"Who swears he'll have me if he can."
Whipsee diddle dee dandy O!
Then Uncle Rat gave his consent
And made a handsome settlement.
With a harum scarum diddle dum darum,
Whipsee diddle dee dandy O!

5. Four partridge pies with season made,
Whipsee diddle dee dandy O!
Two potted larks and marmalade,
Whipsee diddle dee dandy O!
Four woodcocks and a venison pie,
I would that at that feast were I.
With a harum scarum diddle dum darum,
Whipsee diddle dee dandy O!

Hanukah

Jewish Folk Song
Words Adapted

Hanukah is an important holiday for the Jewish people. It lasts eight days.

Over 2,000 years ago foreign invaders captured the temple of the Jews. Hanukah celebrates the return of the Jews to the temple after the invaders had been driven out.

Happily

Drey - dl spin round and round,

Make your mer - ry — whir - ring sound.

Ha - nu - kah brings its joys;

Hap - py are the girls and boys.

One by one, — light each can - dle

At this joy - ous time of year. —

74

As they glow, __ spin the drey - dl;

Ha - nu - kah __ brings its cheer.

Afternoon on a Hill

by Edna St. Vincent Millay

Read this poem with expression.
Learn to say it from memory.

I will be the gladdest thing
    Under the sun!
I will touch a hundred flowers
    And not pick one.
        I will look at cliffs and clouds
           With quiet eyes,
    Watch the wind bow down the grass,
        And the grass rise.
                And when lights begin to show
                Up from the town,
           I will mark which must be mine,
             And then start down!

Plan how you would compose a melody for this poem.
Where would each musical phrase begin and end?
Which phrases of melody would need to soar and swell?
Which phrases would come to rest?
As you read the words, can you tap the rhythm in which your
melody would move?

Compose a melody for one stanza or the whole poem.
Some class members may sing their melodies.
Others may play their melodies on the bells.
Does your melody fit the mood of the words?

The Little Jesus Came to Town

Music by Bonnie Jean Coleman
Words by Lizette Woodworth Reese

Tenderly

1. The lit - tle Je - sus came to town;
2. Then o - pened wide a sta - ble door;

The wind blew up, the wind blew down;
Fair were the rush - es on the floor;

Out in the street the wind was bold;
The ox put forth a horn - èd head:

Now who would house him from the cold?
"Come, lit - tle Lord, here make thy bed."

3. Up rose the sheep were folded near:
   "Thou Lamb of God, come, enter here."
   He entered there to rush and reed,
   Who was the Lamb of God indeed.

4. The little Jesus came to town;
   With ox and sheep he laid him down;
   Peace to the byre and peace to the fold,
   For that they housed him from the cold!

77

Bring a Torch, Jeannette, Isabella

French Carol
Words Adapted

Make a dance drama for this carol. Act out the words as you move toward an imaginary creche. Skip in a happy processional and beckon to the "folk of the village." Let "Jeannette" and "Isabella" be the leaders. Tiptoe around and look at the child.

Lightly

1. Bring a torch, — Jean - nette, Is - a - bel - la,
2. Gent - ly now — the babe — is sleep - ing,

Swift - ly to —— the cra - dle run.
Mar - y rocks — him in —— her arms.

Christ is born, — good folk of the vil - lage,
Come, oh, come — and see him in slum - ber,

Light — a torch that you may see him.
Qui - et - ly now stand by the man - ger.

78

Ah, ah, beau - ti - ful is the moth - er,
Hush, hush, see how he sleeps so sweet - ly,

Ah, ah, beau - ti - ful is the child. ___
Hush, hush, peace - ful - ly sleeps the babe. ___

Christmas Is Here

Danish Round
Words Adapted

1.
Christ - mas is here,

Best time of year,

2.
When we re - mem - ber all our

friends far and near.

I Saw Three Ships

English Carol

Listen to the record. The instruments
that you hear are very ancient. They
were played many, many years ago, when
this song was first sung.

Joyfully

1. I saw three ships come sail - ing in,
2. And what was in those ships all three,

On Christ - mas day, on Christ - mas day,

I saw three ships come sail - ing in,
And what was in those ships all three,

On Christ - mas day in the morn - ing.

3.
Sweet Mary and the Christ were there,
On Christmas day, on Christmas day,
Sweet Mary and the Christ were there,
On Christmas day in the morning.

4.
Pray, whither sailed those ships all three,
On Christmas day, on Christmas day,
Pray, whither sailed those ships all three,
On Christmas day in the morning.

5.
Oh, they sailed into Bethlehem,
On Christmas day, on Christmas day,
Oh, they sailed into Bethlehem,
On Christmas day in the morning.

6.
Then let us all rejoice again,
On Christmas day, on Christmas day,
Then let us all rejoice again,
On Christmas day in the morning.

On the record a choir sings this carol.
A choir combines the voices of many
men and women. Listen for other songs
that are sung by a choir.

O Little Town
of Bethlehem

Music by Lewis H. Redner
Words by Phillips Brooks

Quietly

O lit - tle town of Beth - le - hem, How
still we __ see thee lie. A - bove thy deep and
dream - less sleep, The si - lent __ stars go by;
Yet in thy dark streets shin - eth The
ev - er - last - ing light; The hopes and fears of
all the years Are met in thee to - night.

A Child Was Born
upon This Earth

Compare the recording of this song with
the recording of "I Saw Three Ships."
In what ways are they alike?

Old Dutch Melody
Words Translated

Simply

1. A Child was born up - on this earth,
2. A Child was born for us this day,

A Child was born up - on this earth.
A Child was born for us this day,

He gave __ to each __ of us __ his birth,
His cra - dle a man - ger, his blan - ket of hay,

He gave __ to each __ of us __ his birth.
His cra - dle a man - ger, his blan - ket of hay.

3. A faithful watch the angels kept. *(2 times)*
   They rocked the Child who peacefully slept. *(2 times)*

4. His eyes were black, as black as jet, *(2 times)*
   In rosy cheeks so finely set. *(2 times)*

5. He came on earth for everyone here, *(2 times)*
   And wishes us all a Happy New Year. *(2 times)*

Add this melody pattern on the bells as an accompaniment.

Tap the bell with the hammer softly and rapidly, making the
tone ring all the way through the measure.

'Twas in the Moon of Wintertime

Huron Indian Carol
Words by J. E. Middleton

1. 'Twas in the moon of win - ter -time
2. With - in a lodge of bro - ken bark
3. Ye chil - dren of the for - est free,

when all the birds had fled,
the ten - der Babe was found.
ye sons of Man - i - tou,

That might - y Git - chi Man - i - tou
A rag - ged robe of rab - bit skin
The Ho - ly Child of earth and heav'n

sent an - gel choirs in - stead.
en - wrapped His beau - ty round.
is born to - day for you.

Be - fore their light the stars grew dim,
And as the hunt - er braves drew nigh,
Come kneel be - fore the ra - diant Boy

and won - d'ring hunt - ers heard the hymn:—
the an - gel song rang loud and high:—
who brings you beau - ty, peace, and joy;—

Refrain

Je - sus, your King, is born; Je - sus is

born! *In ex - cel - sis glo - ri - a!*

Christmas Eve

by Marion Edey

On a winter night
When the moon is low
the rabbits hop on the frozen snow.
The woodpecker sleeps in his hole in the tree
And fast asleep is the chickadee.

Twelve o'clock
and the world is still
as the Christmas star comes over the hill.
The angels sing, and sing again:
"Peace on earth, Goodwill to men."

85

This gay carol tells of some of the ways people have celebrated Christmas. When we decorate our houses with holly, we are doing just as boys and girls did in England long ago.

Deck the Halls

Old Welsh Air
Traditional Words

The Yule log was an important part of Christmas. A huge log, large enough to burn for twelve days, was chosen. It was lighted on Christmas Eve and burned all through the holiday.

Gaily

1. Deck the halls with boughs of hol - ly,
2. See the blaz - ing Yule be - fore us,
3. Fast a - way the old year pass - es,

Fa la la la la la la la la.

'Tis the sea - son to be jol - ly,
Strike the harp and join the cho - rus,
Hail the new, ye lads and lass - es,

Fa la la la la la la la la.

86

Don we now our gay ap - par - el,
Fol - low me in mer - ry mea - sure,
Sing we joy - ous all to - geth - er,

Fa la la la la la la la la.

Troll the an - cient Yule - tide car - ol,
While I tell of Yule - tide trea - sure,
Heed - less of the wind and weath - er,

Fa la la la la la la la la.

Music Is Expression

People express their thoughts and feelings in words, pictures,
and movements.
Paintings, statues, poetry, and stories express what the
artist thinks and feels.

Music is expression, too.
A musical composition expresses what the **composer** thinks and
feels.
Musical ideas of the composer often stand alone without
describing anything.
Music can also express a mood or describe a scene.
It can describe the work and play of the people.

We express the thoughts and feelings of the music as we sing,
dance, and play instruments.
We try to understand what the composer and the performers
express through music as we listen.

Vesper Hymn

Music Attributed to
Dmitri Bortniansky
Words by Thomas Moore

"Vesper" hymn means "evening" hymn. "Jubilate" means "rejoice." How does the music help you express the joyful meaning of the words? Which section of the song will you sing louder?

Joyfully

Hark, the ves - per hymn is steal - ing
Near - er yet and near - er peal - ing,

O'er the wa - ters soft and clear.
Soft it breaks up - on the ear.

Ju - bi - la - te! Ju - bi - la - te!

Ju - bi - la - te! A - men.

Add the following accompaniment to suggest evening bells.
Play it on the bells or the piano.

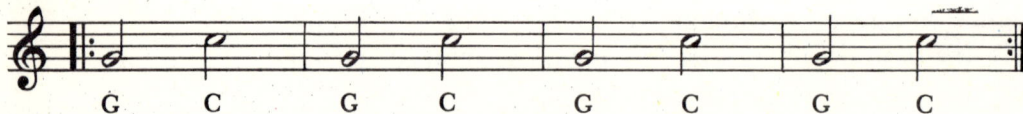

C B C G C B C G

G C G C G C G C

90

The people who sang this song lived on islands off the shore of Georgia. The boat crews made up songs as they rowed to the mainland. Each boat had its own song. The lead oarsman on one boat must have been named Michael.

Michael, Row the Boat Ashore

Spiritual

With feeling

1. Mi - chael, row the boat a - shore,
2. Mi - chael's boat's a mu - sic boat,

Hal - le - lu - jah!
Hal - le - lu - jah!

Mi - chael, row the boat a - shore,
Mi - chael's boat's a mu - sic boat,

Hal - le - lu - jah!
Hal - le - lu - jah!

3. Michael, row the boat ashore, Hallelujah! (2 times)
4. Sister, help to trim the sail, Hallelujah! (2 times)
5. Michael, row the boat ashore, Hallelujah! (2 times)

The Little Sandman

Arranged by Johannes Brahms
Traditional Words

Johannes Brahms was one of the great composers of songs. Why does his melody for this song seem so perfect for a lullaby? How does his accompaniment add to the beauty of the music?

Discuss the reasons why your voice naturally grows louder as you sing the third phrase.

Gently

1. The flow - ers all sleep sound - ly be -
2. Now see, at ev - ery win - dow the

neath_ the moon's_ bright ray; They nod their heads to -
sand - man shows_ his head, And looks for lit - tle

geth - er and dream_ the night_ a - way.
chil - dren who ought_ to be __ in bed.

The __ rus - tling trees wave to and fro
And __ as each wea - ry one he spies,

and __ mur - mur soft and low. }
throws __ sand in - to his eyes. } Sleep __ on,

sleep __ on, __ sleep __ on, my __ lit - tle one.

The __ rus - tling trees wave to and fro
And __ as each wea - ry one he spies,

and __ mur - mur soft and low. }
throws __ sand in - to his eyes. } Sleep __ on,

sleep __ on, __ sleep __ on, my __ lit - tle one.

Night Herding Song

Cowboy Song

Discuss the life of a cowboy. How do the words and music of this song express the cowboy's feelings? How will you sing the song to match that expression?

Easily

F C7 F C7

1. Go slow, lit - tle do - gies, stop mill - in' a - round;
2. Lay down, lit - tle do - gies, and when you've laid down

F C7 F C7

I'm tired of your rov - in' all o - ver the ground.
Just stretch your - selves out for there's plen - ty of ground.

F F C7

There's grass where you're stand - in', so feed kind of slow;
Stay put, lit - tle do - gies, for I'm aw - ful tired;

F C7 F C7

You don't have for - ev - er to be on the go.
If you get a - way I am sure to be fired.

Move slow, lit - tle do - gies, move slow, _____
Lay down, lit - tle do - gies, lay down, _____

Hi - o, hi - o, ___ hi - o. _____

This cowboy call has a purpose. Have you heard other calls or cries as boys sell newspapers or as the vegetable man comes by?

Cowboy's Gettin'-Up Holler

Cowboy Call

Freely

Wake up, Ja - cob, day's a - break- in'; ___

Fry - in' pan's on an' hoe - cake ___ bak- in'.

A Soldier's Tale

by Igor Stravinsky

Composers sometimes tell a story in music. Stravinsky
wrote music to help tell a story called "A Soldier's Tale."
Listen to the record and hear the music that describes three
of the soldier's adventures. The music for each of these
scenes is very different because Stravinsky is describing
three very different adventures.

In the first scene the soldier is walking along the road.
The music suggests a march. You can hear the soldier's
footsteps in the steady rhythm of the double bass. As he
continues his walk, you can hear the drums and tambourine
marking his steps.

In the second scene the soldier stops to rest beside a brook.
The clarinet and the bassoon answer each other in a quiet
duet. Listen for the melody played by the trumpet. The
sound of the instruments suggests a peaceful country scene.

After the teacher has told you the rest of the story,
listen to the music for the third scene. It is called the
"Devil's Dance." Why is it a good title for this music?
How should it be danced? What do you think happens to the
devil at the end of the dance? What instrument helps you
to know?

After you have listened to all the scenes, compare the music
for each. In what ways is the music different for each
scene? Talk about the melodies, the rhythm, the moods, and
the important instruments.

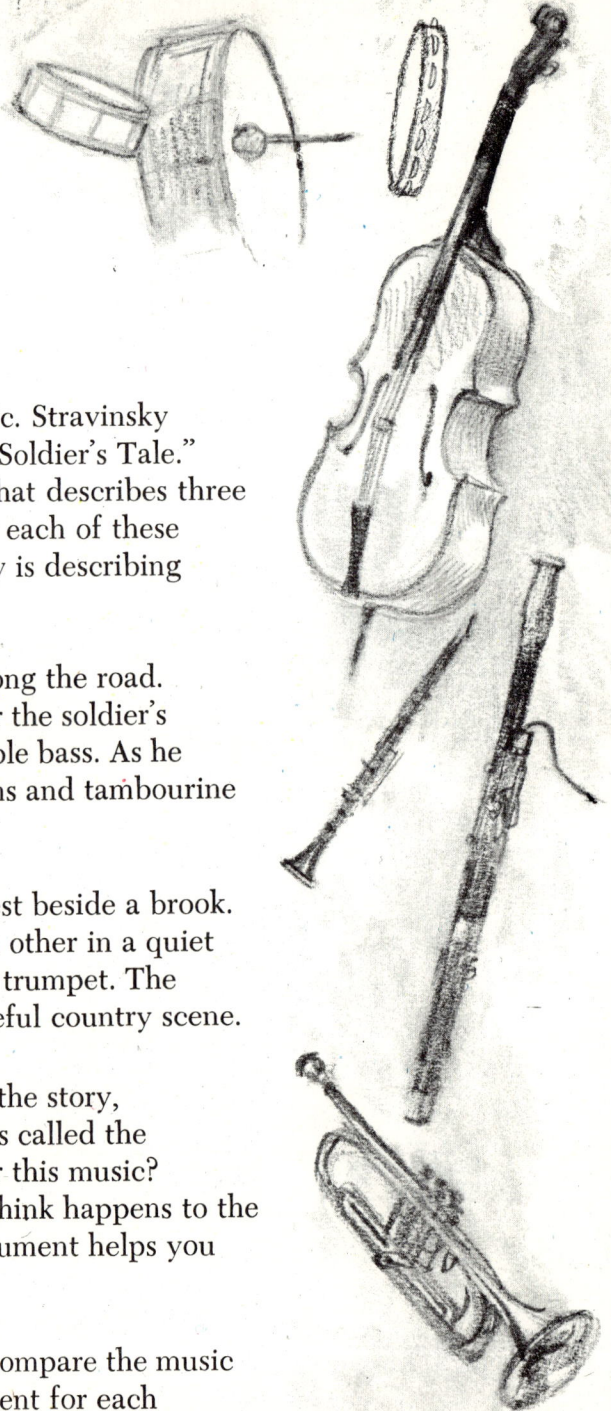

The words of this spinning song have no meaning. They imitate the sound of the spinning wheel. The song is an example of the way in which people sing about their work. Sing lightly and crisply or the words will trip you.

Sarasponda

Dutch Spinning Song

Sa - ra- spon- da, Sa - ra- spon- da, Sa - ra-spon-da, Ret - set- set!

Sa - ra-spon- da, Sa - ra-spon-da, Sa - ra- spon-da, Ret- set- set!

Ah - do - ray - oh!   Ah - do - ray- boom - day - oh!

Ah - do - ray-boom-day, Ret-set- set!   A - say- pa - say- oh!

The boys may sing this chant during the first section of the song:

boom - da, boom - da, boom - da, boom - da

The Star-Spangled Banner

Composer Unknown
Words by Francis Scott Key

Our national anthem is an important song you will sing all your life. What feeling do you have when you sing it? How does the music help you express this feeling?

Oh, __ say, can you see by the dawn's ear - ly light,

What so proud - ly we hailed at the twi - light's last gleam-ing?

Whose broad stripes and bright stars, through the per - il - ous fight,

O'er the ram - parts we watched were so gal - lant - ly stream-ing?

98

And the rock - ets' red glare, the bombs burst-ing in air,

Gave proof through the night that our flag was still there.

Oh, say, does that __ star- span- gled ban - ner __ yet __ wave __

O'er the land __ of the free and the home of the brave?

Sing Together in Assembly

Join with some other classes that know your songs.
Many voices make a beautiful sound.

Here are some songs for an "Autumn Sing."

You can sing these in a "Spring Sing."

When you have learned this song in German, you will know several words which are fun to know and to say.

Weiss sind alle meine Kleider

German Folk Song

1. Weiss, weiss, weiss sind al - le mei - ne Klei - der,
2. Grün, grün, grün sind al - le mei - ne Klei - der,

weiss, weiss, weiss ist al - les, was ich hab.
grün, grün, grün ist al - les, was ich hab.

Da - rum __ lieb ich al - les, was so weiss ist,
Da - rum __ lieb ich al - les, was so grün ist,

weil mein Schatz ein Bäk - ker, Bäk - ker ist.
weil mein Schatz ein Jä - ger, Jä - ger ist.

3. Schwarz, schwarz, schwarz sind alle meine Kleider,
   schwarz, schwarz, schwarz ist alles, was ich hab.
   Darum lieb ich alles, was so schwarz ist,
   weil mein Schatz ein Schornsteinfeger ist. } *(2 times)*

4. Bunt, bunt, bunt sind alle meine Kleider,
   bunt, bunt, bunt ist alles, was ich hab.
   Darum lieb ich alles, was so bunt ist,
   weil mein Schatz ein Maler, Maler ist. } *(2 times)*

101

Home on the Range

Cowboy Song

1. Oh, give me a home where the buf - fa - lo roam,
2. How of - ten at night when the heav - ens are bright

Where the deer and the an - te - lope play, _____
With the lights from the glit - ter - ing stars, _____

Where sel - dom is heard a dis - cour - ag - ing word,
Have I stood there a - mazed and _____ asked as I gazed

And the skies are not cloud - y all day.
If their glo - ry ex - ceeds that of ours.

Refrain

Home,   home on   the   range, _____

Where the deer   and the an - te - lope play, _____

Where sel - dom is   heard   a dis - cour - ag - ing word,

And the skies   are not cloud - y   all   day. _____

Hailstones and Halibut Bones

from *Adventures in Color*
by Mary O'Neill

Like acrobats on a high trapeze
The Colors pose and bend their knees
Twist and turn and leap and blend
Into shapes and feelings without end—

Black is the night
When there isn't a star
And you can't tell by looking
Where you are.

The sound of black is
"Boom! Boom! Boom!"
Echoing in
An empty room.

Blue is the color of the sky
Without a cloud
Cool, distant, beautiful
And proud.

And if you listen
You can hear blue
In wind over water
And wherever flax blooms
And when evening steps into
Lonely rooms.

White is the sound
Of a light foot walking
White is a pair of
Whispers talking.

Red is a sunset
Blazy and bright.
Red is feeling brave
With all your might.
Red is a lipstick
Red is a shout,
Red is a signal
That says: "Watch out!"

Red is a show-off
No doubt about—
But can you imagine
Living without it?

Green is the grass
And the leaves of trees
Green is the smell
Of a country breeze.

Green is an olive
And a pickle.
The sound of green
Is a water-trickle.
Green is the world
After the rain
Bathed and beautiful
Again.

Choose music that expresses the same moods suggested by these
stanzas. Make a melody using your favorite color. Does it suggest
a special feeling? Write a poem describing another color.

Al Hasela

Hasidic Tune
Biblical Text

This Jewish song is not a laughing song, as you might think! "Haḥ" in Hebrew means "hit." The pioneers in Israel sang this happy work song as they hewed rock. "Al hasela" means "on the rocks." "V'yetsu mayim hayim" means "fresh water gushes forth."

This song is a good example of the way in which people express their feeling in music.

Joyously

Al ha - se - la haḥ, haḥ, al ha - se - la

haḥ, haḥ, haḥ, Al ha - se - la haḥ, haḥ, v'

1.
2.

yë - tsu ma - yim ha - yim, ha - yim.___

La la la la la la la la

la La la la la la haḥ, haḥ, haḥ,

106

la la la la la hah, hah, hah, La la

la la la la la la la la la la la.

Dance the Hora

The **hora** is a Jewish circle dance which is a part of all festive occasions. Many tunes are used. The steps are always the same. The Greeks also do this dance with their folk tunes. The tune on your record is called "Ali, Ali."

To take your places for the dance, stand in a single circle, facing center, hands joined. The dance is done in short weaving steps around the circle, feet crossing with hops. The dance is easier and prettier if you dance in bare feet.

Music Has Design

Design is the plan of music.
Design gives music **order** and **balance.**
Without design musical tones would go on and on, giving us a feeling of confusion.
Order and balance give us a feeling of satisfaction.

Repeated melodies and new melodies are a part of design.
The new melodies are introduced for variety.

We can write the design of music by giving letter names to the melodies.
A song may have one of these designs:

A   B   A
A   B   A   C
A   A   B   A

A piece for orchestra may also have one of these designs, although the melodies are usually longer.

Can you find the design of music you know?

Skater's Waltz

Music by Emil Waldteufel
Words Adapted

This song was first written as a waltz to be played by an orchestra. Later, words were added. Listen to the recording of the waltz. The first section is written here for you to see. Call it by the letter name "A." Can you write the design with letters for the rest of the waltz? How does the composer give variety to his music?

Skat - ing a - way, _____ Glide,

glide and sway, _____ Life's filled with

glee On a win - ter day. _____

After you have listened to the waltz several times, you may enjoy singing these words to the melody that is not written in your book.

Fingers are tingling and good friends are mingling as
Snowflakes are swirling and cool breezes whirling and
Children are singing and sleigh bells are ringing as
Round we go!

110

Plan an accompaniment
which would suggest
the sounds described in the song.

Winter Weather

Russian Folk Melody
Words by Ivan Petrovsky

Briskly

Come a - long in win - ter weath - er,

Come and join me in a sleigh.

Hear the sleigh bells ring - ing, jin - gling,

Feel the wind __ as we dash a - way.

Now we go o - ver ice and snow __ to the

stead - y trot - ting of the hoofs be - low.

Oh, Dear! What Can the Matter Be?

Listen to the recording of this song. When does the clarinet play the melody?

English Folk Song

Jauntily

Refrain

Oh, dear! What can the mat - ter be?

Dear, dear, what can the mat - ter be?

Oh, dear! What can the mat - ter be?

Fine

John - ny's so long at the fair. _____

Verse

1. He prom-ised to bring me a trin-ket to please me,
2. He prom-ised to bring me a bas-ket of po-sies,

And then for a smile, oh, he vowed he would tease me;
A gar-land of lil-ies, a gar-land of ros-es,

He prom-ised to bring me a bunch of blue rib-bons
A lit-tle straw hat to set off the blue rib-bons

D.C. al Fine

To tie up my bon-nie brown hair.____ And it's
That tie up my bon-nie brown hair.____ And it's

Children's Symphony
Second Movement

By Harl McDonald

A symphony is played by a **symphony orchestra.**
A symphony is a long piece of music which has large sections
or **movements.**
One movement may be vigorous, one slow, one lively, to give
variety.
The composer called this composition *Children's Symphony*
because he used children's songs as his themes.

Listen to the second movement of the symphony.
It is called the **slow** movement.
Name the songs that you recognize.
How did the composer achieve variety in the movement?
Listen again and tell all that you noticed.

These are the two main themes:

What gives order and balance to this
song? Can you write the design
with letters?

Come Tend the Geese

Czech Folk Song
Words Adapted

1. Come lit - tle girl now and tend the geese; they've
2. Did you not hear the wind blow last night? It

all run a - way. Did you not know that the
moaned and it sighed. It blew the latch from the

barn - yard gate is o - pen to - day?
barn - yard gate and o - pened it wide.

Since the break of the morn, geese have

been in the corn. Come lit - tle girl now and

tend your geese be - fore it's too late.

Love Somebody

American Folk Song

1. Love some-bod-y, yes I do,
2. Love some-bod-y, can't guess who,

Love some-bod-y, yes I do,
Love some-bod-y, can't guess who,

Love some-bod-y, yes I do,
Love some-bod-y, can't guess who,

Love some-bod-y but I won't tell who.
Love some-bod-y but I won't tell who.

Refrain

Love some - bod - y, yes I do,

Love some - bod - y, yes I do,

Love some - bod - y, yes I do, And I

hope some - bod - y loves me too.

3. Love somebody's eyes of blue, *(3 times)*
   Love somebody but I won't tell who.
   Refrain

4. Love somebody's smile so true, *(3 times)*
   Love somebody but I won't tell who.
   Refrain

This song uses the same melody and rhythm patterns over and over again. Add interest by playing a descant on the bells. Make up words so that you can sing the descant.

E C B   E C D   E C F   E D C

E C E   E C D   E C E   E D C

Down the River

American Play-Party Song

Vigorously

1. The riv - er is up, and the chan - nel is deep,
2. The riv - er is up, and the chan - nel is deep,

The wind is stead - y and strong; ____
The wind is stead - y and strong; ____

Oh, won't we have a jol - ly good time
The waves do splash from shore ____ to shore

As we go sail - ing a - long.
As we go sail - ing a - long.

Refrain

Down the riv - er, oh, down the riv - er, Oh,

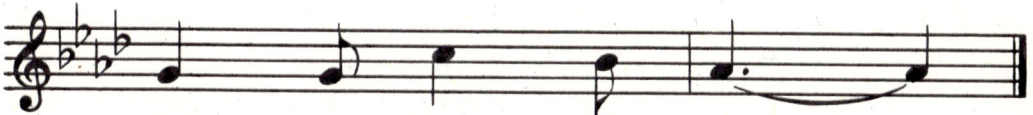

down the riv - er we go - o - o!

Down the riv - er, oh, down the riv - er, Oh,

down the O - hi - o! _____

Phrases in a song sometimes are grouped together to form larger sections. This song has two sections. How many phrases are in each section? Listen carefully to the endings of the phrases. Which endings make you feel that the song should go on? Which ones come to rest?

Chebogah
(Beetle)

Hungarian Folk Dance
Words Adapted

Hungarian folk songs often are
accompanied by string instruments.
See if you can name one string
instrument that you hear on the
record.

With spirit

In a cir-cle slide to left and don't be slow.
For-ward with a walk-ing step, then back in place.

To the right we slide a-gain as back we go.
Skip with el-bows joined and then your part-ner face.

Side-ward glide, side-ward glide, to the cen-ter glide;
Fast-er now, fast-er now, fast-er in and out;

Back a-gain, back a-gain, part-ners side by side.
Part-ners swing, part-ners swing, end-ing with a shout. *Hey!*

The words tell you how to dance to this song.
Notice how the design of the dance changes with the design of
the music.

Susy, Little Susy

German Folk Song
Words Adapted

Su - sy, lit - tle Su - sy, pray what is the news?

The geese are go - ing bare - foot be - cause they've no shoes.

The cob - bler has leath - er but no last to use,

So he can - not make them a new pair of shoes.

"Susy, Little Susy" is a German folk song which the composer
Engelbert Humperdinck used in his opera *Hansel and Gretel*.
"Hansel and Gretel" is a German folk tale known to boys and
girls the world over. Humperdinck used the story for his
opera, which is almost as well known as the original tale.
"Brother, Come and Dance with Me" and "Little Man in the
Wood," which appear on the next pages, are also used in the
opera. You will enjoy knowing all three songs.

121

Brother, Come and Dance with Me

German Folk Song
Words Adapted

Gretel: Broth-er, come and dance with me, Both my hands I give to thee,

Right foot first, left foot then, Round a - bout and back a - gain.

Hansel: I would dance but don't know how, When to clap and when to bow;

Show me what I ought to do So that I may dance with you.

Gretel: With your feet go tap, tap, tap, With your hands go clap, clap, clap,
Both: With your head go nick, nick, nick, With your fin - gers click, click, click,

Right foot first, left foot then, Round a - bout and back a - gain.
Right foot first, left foot then, Round a - bout and back a - gain.

Little Man in the Wood

German Folk Song
Words Adapted

There stands a lit - tle man in the deep, dark wood;

He wears a pur - ple coat and a small, black hood.

Tell me who this man can be, stand - ing there so si - lent - ly,

In his pur - ple coat ___ and a small, black hood?

Hansel and Gretel

an Opera

by Engelbert Humperdinck

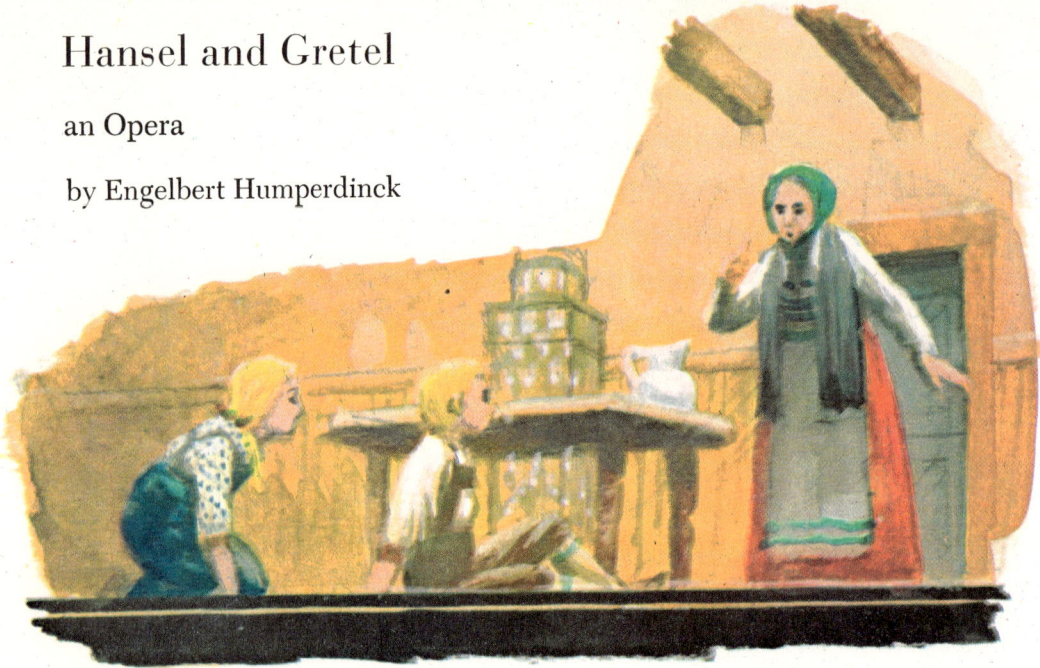

Act One

Act One takes place in the mountain cottage of the family. The
father and mother have gone to sell brooms in the village. We
see Hansel and Gretel alone in the little room.

As Hansel works at making a broom, Gretel knits a stocking and
sings "Susy, Little Susy." Soon the hungry children grow tired
of their work and begin to romp around. They amuse themselves by
dancing, and Gretel teaches Hansel as they sing "Brother, Come
and Dance with Me."

Their play becomes more boisterous until, finally, they go
tumbling over one another. Suddenly they are surprised by their
mother, who returns weary and sad because she has not been able
to sell the brooms. As she scolds the children, she spills their
only food, a pitcher of milk. In her anger she sends Hansel and
Gretel to the woods to pick strawberries. Not until their father
returns and reminds her of the witch, does the mother remember
the great danger her children face alone in the woods.

124

Act Two

In Act Two we see a stage setting which resembles a deep forest
in Germany. The children have filled their basket with berries.
As they sit on the ground, Gretel weaves a garland of wild flowers.
She sees a jack-in-the-pulpit growing beside her and describes it
in her song, "Little Man in the Wood."

The orchestra plays sounds of the woods at night with the cries
of cuckoos and owls. We realize that the children are lost and
frightened. As night descends they kneel to sing one of the
finest songs in the opera, "The Evening Prayer." As they finish
the song and fall asleep, the orchestra plays the melody again.
We see the angels descend and stand beside the children, then
ascend again into heaven. This is one of the most beautiful
scenes in the opera.

Evening Prayer

When at night I go to sleep, Fourteen angels watch do keep,
Two my head are guarding, Two my feet are guiding,
Two are on my right hand, Two are on my left hand,
Two who warmly cover, Two who o'er me hover,
Two to whom 'tis given To guide my steps to Heaven.

Act Three

When the curtain opens for Act Three, we see the Dew Fairy
shaking dew drops from a bluebell on the sleeping children.
He sings the "Dew Fairy's Song."

I'm up with early dawning, And know who loves the morning,
Who'll rise fresh as a daisy, Who'll sink in the slumber lazy,
    ding! dong! ding! dong!
And with the golden light of day I chase the fading night away,
Fresh dew around me shaking, And hill and dale awaking;
Then up, with all your powers Enjoy the morning hours,
The scent of trees and flowers, Then up, ye sleepers awaken!
The rosy dawn is smiling, Then up, ye sleepers, awake, awake!

The children awaken and sing merrily with the joy of a new day.

Suddenly the children notice a little house built of good things to
eat. It is, alas, the house of the wicked witch who traps boys
and girls by her spells and bakes them into gingerbread. As
Hansel and Gretel break off tasty morsels from the house, the old
witch appears and begins to work her hocus-pocus on them.

126

When she has succeeded in getting Gretel into a cage, the witch rides her broomstick in wild delight.

The orchestra plays wonderful music for the witch's ride, and the witch sings:

> So hop, hop, hop, gallop, lop, lop!
> My broomstick nag, come do not lag!
> At dawn of day I ride away,
> Am here and there and everywhere!
> At midnight hour, when none can know,
> To join the witches' dance I go!

If you know the folk tale, you will remember that Hansel and Gretel are very clever. Soon they manage to free themselves, shove the witch into the oven, and slam the door shut. They dance gleefully as their parents arrive to join in the celebration. The gingerbread children around the witch's house become real boys and girls again, and all join in the joyous dance and chorus of thanksgiving.

Now that you know many of the songs and the action of the opera, you are ready to study the beautiful composition which the orchestra plays before the curtain opens. It is called the "overture," which means "opening." Humperdinck composed it by using melodies and rhythms which are sung and played in the opera.

The overture prepares us for the exciting moment when we see the stage setting and hear the first words as the characters begin to sing and act.

The overture begins with the melody of the "Evening Prayer." We hear the mysterious tones of the French horns. The strings and woodwinds join in to finish the melody.

Next we hear the trumpets sounding out the tones which seem to say "hocus-pocus," reminding us of the witch. The hocus-pocus rhythm is repeated in many different ways. Can you hear them?

Much of the overture is based on the joyful music near the end
of the opera when the gingerbread children dance and sing.
If you listen carefully, you will hear their song of thanks to
Hansel and Gretel and their dance which begins "the spell is
broke."

We hear the melodies combined in an exciting section. Finally
the peaceful "Prayer" returns, and the audience feels the mood
with which the story begins.

Music Combines Tones

In music, tones are combined to make **harmony.**
You hear harmony when two or more tones are sounded together.

Listen for the harmony your voices make when you sing **rounds.**
Listen for other ways in which music combines tones
    as you play instruments with your singing,
    as you hear your song records and notice the accompaniments,
    as you hear the instruments of the band and orchestra.

You are learning to listen carefully as you sing, play, and hear
music.
You know **rhythm** in music.
You know **melody.**
You can also learn to sing, play, and hear **harmony.**

Are You Sleeping?

Frère Jacques

French Folk Tune
Traditional Words

"Are You Sleeping?" is a round which people sing in many lands. You will enjoy singing it in French as well as in English. Learn the song very well before you sing it as a two-part round. Listen to the record and hear the instruments and voices combine to make harmony. Listen to the harmony of your voices as you sing "round and round."

1. **F**   **F**

Are   you   sleep - ing,   are   you   sleep - ing,
Frè - re   Jac - ques,   Frè - re   Jac - ques,

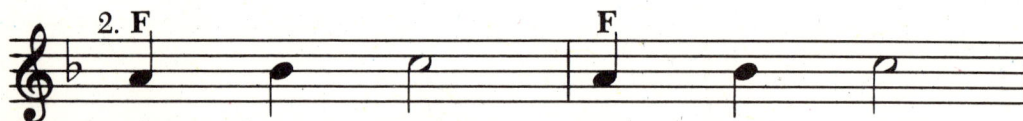

2. **F**   **F**

Broth - er   John,   Broth - er   John?
Dor - mez - vous,   dor - mez - vous?

F   **F**

Morn - ing bells are ring - ing, morn - ing bells are ring - ing,
Son - nez les ma - ti - nes, son - nez les ma - ti - nes,

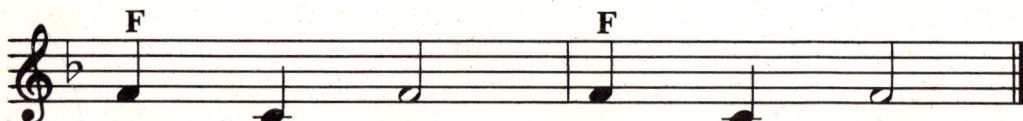

F   **F**

Ding,   ding,   dong,   ding,   ding,   dong.
Din,   din,   don,   din,   din,   don.

132

Three Blind Mice

Traditional Round

Three blind mice, ___ three blind mice, ___

See how they run, ___ see how they run! ___

They all ran af - ter the farm - er's wife,

She cut off their tails with a carv - ing knife;

Did ev - er you see such a sight in your life

As three blind mice?

The Wise Old Owl

Here is a three-part round for you to enjoy.

Traditional Round

The wise old owl sat in an oak,

The more he heard, the less he spoke,

The more he heard, the less he spoke.

You will enjoy singing as rounds these songs that you already know:

134

This gay Jewish folk song celebrates
Arbor Day, which comes much earlier in
the year in Israel than it does in
the United States.

Arbor Day Song

Israeli Folk Song
Words Adapted

Gaily

Young and old are sing - ing, young and old are sing - ing,

La la la la la la la la la la la, While

plant - ing, sow - ing, cut - ting, reap - ing, Young and old are sing - ing,

La la la la la la la la, Young and old are sing - ing,

La la la la la la la la, Young and old are sing - ing.

Sing in harmony by repeating the first two measures of the song over
and over as a chant. Sing the chant using "la."

Canzona No. 2 for Brass and Organ

by Giovanni Gabrieli

In the "Canzona No. 2 for Brass and Organ" the voices of two trumpets, two trombones, and organ are heard in harmony. The voices of instruments combine to make harmony. Your voices combine to make harmony as you sing rounds.

"Canzona" means song. This canzona is for brass instruments. The trumpet and the trombone are brass instruments.

In the opening section, a trumpet introduces the main theme. The other brass instruments enter, one by one. Each imitates the trumpet's theme in the same way one voice imitates another in a round.

The middle section sounds like a conversation between the brass instruments and the organ. The organ begins the conversation with a musical phrase which is answered by the trumpets. Then the brass instruments begin a new phrase and the organ replies. In the next part can you hear a short conversation between the trumpets and the trombones?

Listen for the exciting ending in which the organ and brasses all play together. Have you heard the melody of this section earlier in this music?

You have often made up your own
accompaniments on the bells. Listen
to the record and hear the bell
accompaniment to this song. Now see
if you can play it. Use these
bells: B, C.

Rich Man, Poor Man

American Nonsense Song

1. The rich man sleeps on a feath - er bed
2. The rich man goes in a car - riage fine;
3. The june bug has pret - ty gold - en wings,

With silk - en sheets of blue.
Big let - ters spell his name.
The light - ning bug the flame.

The poor man makes a pal - let
The poor man goes a - walk - ing
The bed - bug does not have wings

But sleeps the whole night through.
But gets there just the same.
But gets there just the same.

You can add **harmony** to your songs by playing an accompaniment on the
autoharp. When you press a button on the autoharp and stroke the
strings, you are playing a **chord.** What is the difference between a
chord and a melody?

Cherry Bloom

Japanese Folk Song
Words Adapted

Listen to the record. Notice the interesting sounds of the **koto.** Japanese folk songs are often accompanied by this ancient string instrument.

Gently

Cher - ry bloom, cher - ry bloom,
Sa - ku - ra Sa - ku - ra

Gent - ly sway - ing in the air,
Ya - yo - i no so - ra wa

Sweet the fra - grance ev - ery - where,
Mi - wa - ta - su ka - gi - ri

Pet - als soft and col - ors bright,
Ka - su - mi ka ku - mo ka

Float - ing clouds that seem to say:
Ni - o - i zo i - zu - ru

Come and see, come and see,
I - za ya I - za ya

Come and see the cher - ry bloom.
Mi ___ ni ___ yu - ka - un

Find the G and A♭ strings on the autoharp and pluck the following pattern to imitate the sound of a Japanese koto. Perhaps someone in the class plays a violin. He could pluck the notes of the accompaniment on his instrument also.

G   A♭   G   A♭

The Magic Garden

Words and Music by
Donald Jenni

Listen to the recording of this song, and notice the accompaniment. Much of the beauty of the song is in its harmony. Can you see and hear something in the rhythm of this song that is different from most of the songs in your book?

Smoothly flowing

Swal - low, swal - low in the sky, may I

fol - low you as you fly to the

mag - ic gar - den? Swal - low, swal -

- low, not so high! You fly fast - er than

I can climb to the mag - ic gar - den.

Composers of today look for ways of "being free" as they express musical ideas. They often break away from the usual ways of writing music. Notice how the composer creates a song which is free by using three different meters. Look for three different meter signatures. By using different meters, the composer changes the accent to fit the flowing movement of the words.

Wishes

by Norman Ault

What do you look for, what do you seek?
    A silver bird with a golden beak.

What do you long for, what do you crave?
    Golden gems in a silver cave.

What do you lack, and what do you need?
    A silver sword and a golden steed.

What do you want, of what do you dream?
    A golden ship on a silver stream.

What do you have, and what do you own?
    A silver robe and a golden crown.

What would you be? Oh, what would you be?
    Only the king of the land and the sea.

At the Gate of Heaven

Spanish-American Folk Song
Words Adapted

Serenely

1. At the gate of Heav'n ti - ny shoes they are giv - ing
2. An - gel choirs in Heav'n with their voic - es are bring - ing

To the lit - tle bare - foot-ed an - gels there liv - ing.
Joy - ous songs of love all for thee they are sing - ing.

Refrain

Slum - ber, my lit - tle one, slum - ber, my lit - tle one,

Slum - ber, my ni - ño, a - rru, a - rru.

Sometimes **harmony** is created by adding a second melody above the main tune. This second melody is called a **descant.** Here is a descant for you to play on the bells.

142

Play Your Own Harmony

You can make interesting harmony of your own.
It is easy to harmonize a song that uses only the five tones
of the **pentatonic scale.**
You can create harmony by playing any of these five tones as
an accompaniment.
You may play them in any order you choose.

"Old MacDonald Had a Farm" is based on the pentatonic scale.
Play the melody on the black keys of the piano. Start on G flat.

While one class member plays the melody, another may create
harmony by playing an accompaniment on the black keys.
Experiment using just two tones, then three or more.
Play your pattern in different rhythms.
Several children may play accompaniments at the same time.
One may play the piano below the melody, another above.
A third child may play on the bells. Each can play his own
pattern.

More Music to Explore

Your musical explorations have taken you along many paths.
You have sung, played accompaniments, danced, and listened
carefully as you searched for musical treasures.
Do you have favorite ways of exploring?

Some of the clues helped you understand more of rhythm and melody.
Some helped you hear combined tones and discover design
and expression in music.
Exploring music is an adventure that never ends.

As you explore more music, see how many clues you will be able
to discover for yourself.

1. Can you find the clue that tells how the song will move
   and which note moves with the beat?
2. Can you find the important rhythm and melody patterns
   in a new song?
3. Can you find the design of a song and write it with
   letters?
4. Can you hear whether a song is in major or minor?
5. Can you plan a rhythm pattern to play as an accompaniment?
6. As you listen to your song records, can you describe
   the accompaniments you hear?
7. As you listen to music, can you discover what gives it
   variety?

There's a Little Wheel A-Turnin'

American Folk Song

Can you answer questions 1, 2, and 3 on page 145? Finding the answers to these questions will help you learn any new song.

1. There's a lit - tle wheel a-turn-in' in my heart,___
2. There's a lit - tle song a-sing-in' in my heart,___

There's a lit - tle wheel a-turn-in' in my heart,
There's a lit - tle song a-sing-in' in my heart,

In my heart,_____ in my heart,_____
In my heart,_____ in my heart,_____

There's a lit - tle wheel a-turn-in' in my heart.
There's a lit - tle song a-sing-in' in my heart.

Some of the class may sing this pattern as a chant.
Sing the chant several times before the rest of the class joins
in singing the melody.

wheel a - turn - in' wheel a - turn - in'

The recording of this song uses a **flute** to suggest the sounds of birds. Can you describe the tone of this **woodwind** instrument?

As you study this song on different days, answer the questions on page 145.

Coming of Spring

German Folk Song
Traditional Words

Joyfully

1. All the birds are here a - gain; Lis - ten to their
2. All the birds are here a - gain; Lis - ten to their

sing - ing, Chirp - ing, war - bling, all day — through,
sing - ing. Rob - in, star - ling, thrush, and — lark,

Sing - ing hap - py songs to — you; Spring will soon be
Twit - ter - ing from dawn to — dark, Wish - ing you a

com - ing — too, Joy and mu - sic bring - ing.
hap - py — year, What a mer - ry greet - ing.

The Four Seasons
First Movement, "Spring"

by Antonio Vivaldi

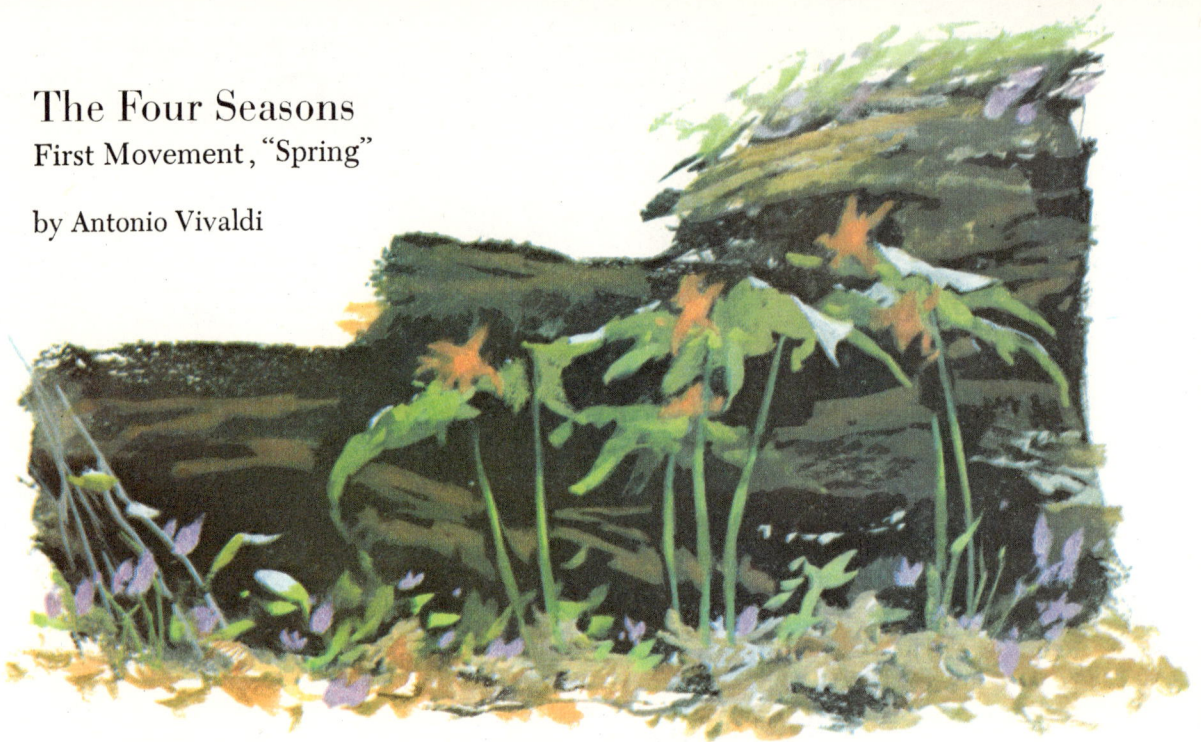

This beautiful music describing spring was composed and
played in Italy when America was still a very primitive
country. It is played as a violin solo accompanied by
other violins and cellos.

Vivaldi was a violinist as well as a composer, and he knew
how to write music which shows off the sounds of the
instrument. He wrote the music in five sections: A, B,
C, D, E. Each section is based on a line of poetry.
Listen to the musical description of the poetry at the
opening of each section.

A   Joyful spring has arrived!
B   The birds welcome it with their songs.
C   The fountains and gentle breezes murmur softly.
D   The sky has a ceiling of black.
        Thunder and lightning announce a storm.
E   When the storm is over, the birds take up their
        enchanting songs.

148

This lovely melody comes to us from the Philippine Islands. One of the authors of your book wrote the Easter words. Sing these words at Easter time. Change some of the words and sing the song at other times.

Dove's Alleluya

Philippine Folk Song
Words by Beth Landis

Delicately

1. A dain-ty dove a-top the spire
2. The bells rang out the joy-ous news

Be-held the earth on Eas-ter morn
For all to sing in hymns of praise;

And sweet-ly sang Al-le-lu-ya,
The dain-ty dove cooed her re-frain:

Al-le-lu-ya, Al-le-lu-ya.

The Cuckoo and the Donkey

Der Kuckuck und der Esel

Music by Karl Friedrich Zelter
German Words by H. von Fallersleben
English Words Adapted

You will enjoy singing this song as the children in Germany sing it. Listen to the recording to learn how to pronounce the German words.

Playfully

1. The cuck - oo and the don - key
2. The cuck - oo start - ed sing - ing;
3. And then they sang to - geth - er;

Were ar - gu - ing one day
The don - key then did bray.
It sound - ed far and near,

Whose ___ voice was best for sing - ing,
They ___ sang a - bout the spring - time,
The ___ don - key with his bray - ing,

150

Whose __ voice was best for sing - ing,
They __ sang a - bout the spring - time,
The __ don - key with his bray - ing,

To wel - come in the spring, ___
A - bout the month of May, ___
The cuck - oo's voice so clear: ___

To wel - come in the spring.
A - bout the month of May.
Cuck - oo, cuck - oo, he - haw.

1. Der Kuckuck und der Esel,
   Die hatten einen Streit,
   Wer wohl am besten sänge *(2 times)*
   Zur schönen Maienzeit. *(2 times)*

2. Der Kuckuck sprach: das kann ich,
   Und fing gleich an zu schrein.
   Ich aber kann es besser! *(2 times)*
   Fiel gleich der Esel ein. *(2 times)*

3. Das klang so schön und lieblich,
   So schön von fern und nah!
   Sie sangen alle beide, *(2 times)*
   Kuckuck, kuckuck, iaaa. *(2 times)*

The Tailor and the Mouse

The answers to questions 1, 2, 3, and 4 on page 145 are important clues which will help you learn this song.

English Folk Song

1. There was a tai - lor had a mouse,
2. The tai - lor thought the mouse was ill,

Hi did - dle un - kum fee - dle.

They lived to - geth - er in one house,
He gave him part of a blue pill,

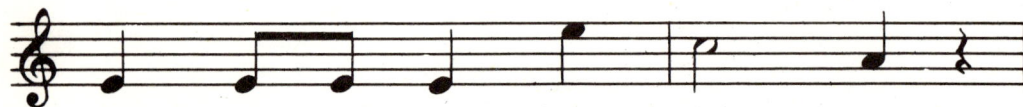

Hi did - dle un - kum fee - dle.

Refrain

Hi did - dle un - kum ta - rum tan - tum,

Through the town of Ram - say,

Hi did - dle un - kum, o - ver the lea,

Hi did - dle un - kum fee - dle.

3. The tailor thought his mouse would die,
Hi diddle unkum feedle.
He baked him in an apple pie.
Hi diddle unkum feedle.
Refrain

4. The pie was cut, the mouse ran out,
Hi diddle unkum feedle.
The tailor followed him all about,
Hi diddle unkum feedle.
Refrain

5. The tailor found his mouse was dead,
Hi diddle unkum feedle.
So he caught another in his stead,
Hi diddle unkum feedle.
Refrain

I Can't Do That Sum

Music by Victor Herbert
Words by Glen MacDonough

When you have learned this song, follow the suggestion in question 5 on page 145. Listen to the recording. Is this accompaniment like the accompaniment you planned? In what ways is it different?

Put down six and car - ry two, Put down six, car - ry two! Gee, but this is hard to do, Hard to do, hard to do! You can think and think and think Till your brains are numb! I don't care what teach - er says, I can't do that sum.

New Sounds in Music

Although music is as old as man, there are still new musical sounds to be discovered.
People continue to explore new ways of making music with new and old instruments.
They explore new kinds of melody, new patterns of rhythm, and new ways to combine tones.

On these pages you will study compositions by present-day composers and find suggestions for making new music of your own.

Toccata for Percussion

Third Movement
by Carlos Chavez

Carlos Chavez is a present-day composer from Mexico.
In this composition he experimented with new ways of making music with percussion instruments alone.
Listen to the record and hear the different instruments.
How many can you name?

Listen for the interesting and exciting patterns of rhythm.
Can you also hear a kind of melody?
How is this possible?

Banshee

by Henry Cowell

Henry Cowell was an American composer who explored new
ways of making music. He created new and interesting
musical sounds in his compositions. He did this by
suggesting new ways to play familiar instruments.

Listen to "Banshee," a composition written for the piano.
In this composition the pianist plays on the strings of the
piano instead of on the keys. He scratches, plucks, and
sweeps the strings with his fingers. A banshee is a ghost.
Why is this a good title for the composition?

Explore ways of making new musical sounds on the autoharp.
Experiment with different kinds of picks to stroke the
strings.
Pluck the strings. Tap them with your hand, a piece of
paper, or a soft bell mallet.
Put a piece of paper under the bars. Then sweep the strings
with your hand.
Plan a short composition using several of the most
interesting sounds you have discovered.

New Music of Your Own

Place these bells in a row to make a pentatonic scale: C, D, E, G, A, C.
With these tones, compose a melody for this verse:

Sun low in the west ....
Moon floating up in the east ....
Flowers in shadow ....

Practice your song until you can remember it.
Compose an accompaniment using the same tones from another set of bells.
Play the tones in any order you like.
Experiment with different rhythms.

Place these bells in a row: C, D, E, F$^\sharp$, G$^\sharp$, A$^\sharp$.
Compose a new melody with these tones.
Give your melody a good design.
When you find a melody you like, play it until you can remember it.

Make your own composition for percussion.
One member of the class may play a drum in a rhythm he likes.
Another drummer may begin later on his drum with his own idea.
Listen for the pattern the drums make together. Other instruments may be added.

Jig Along Home

Words and Music by
Woody Guthrie

The composer of this song loved folk music. He spent much of his life listening to and singing the songs of the American people. The songs he wrote are like the songs he learned from the people as he traveled across the country.

Jauntily

1. I went to the dance and the an - i - mals come;

The jay - bird danced with horse - shoes on.

The grass - hop-per danced till he fell on the floor!

Jig a - long, jig a - long, jig a - long home.

Refrain

Jig jig - a jig jig - a jig a - long home,

Jig jig - a jig jig - a jig a - long home,

Jig a - long, jig a - long, jig a - long home,

Jig jig - a jig jig - a jig a - long home.

2. Fishing worm danced the fishing reel;
   Lobster danced on the peacock's tail.
   Baboon danced with the rising moon!
   Jig along, jig along, jig along home.
   Refrain

3. Mama rat took off her hat,
   Shook the house with the old tom cat.
   The alligator beat his tail on the drum!
   Jig along, jig along, jig along home.
   Refrain

4. The boards did rattle and the house did shake;
   The clouds did laugh and the earth did quake.
   New moon rattled some silver spoons!
   Jig along, jig along, jig along home.
   Refrain

5. The nails flew loose and the floors broke down;
   Everybody danced around and around.
   The house came down and the crowd went home!
   Jig along, jig along, jig along home.
   Refrain

Once More the Winter's Left Us

Old Dutch Melody
Words Translated

Gladly

Once more the win - ter's left _____ us,

I hear the spar - row's song. I see the bud - ding

tu - lips, the spring - time's wel - come throng.

In the qui - et fra - grant __ val - ley, to

lin - ger I de - sire; At eve the song of

night - in - gales, at dawn the feath - ered choir.

From *Folksongs and Games from Holland* by Ann E. Roeder, Copyright 1951, by G. Schirmer, Inc. Used by permission.

Classified Index

American Folk Songs and Spirituals

At the Gate of Heaven, 142
Blow Ye Winds, 12
Cowboy's Gettin'-Up Holler, 95
Deaf Woman's Courtship, 68
Down the River, 118
Four in a Boat, 47
Frog and the Mouse, The, 72
Get on Board, 26
Hawaiian Boat Song, 44
Home on the Range, 102
Love Somebody, 116
Michael, Row the Boat Ashore, 91
Needle's Eye, The, 42
Night Herding Song, 94
Rich Man, Poor Man, 137
Sandy Land, 32
There's a Little Wheel
  A-Turnin', 146
Three Blind Mice, 133
Turn the Glasses Over, 30
You Shall Reap, 22

Animals

Ah, Poor Bird, 69
Alouette, 10
Come Tend the Geese, 115
Coming of Spring, 147
Cuckoo and the Donkey, The, 150
Dove's Alleluya, 149
Frog and the Mouse, The, 72
Jig Along Home, 158
Magic Garden, The, 140
My Farm, 40
Nonsense Song, 11
Ship A-Sailing, 56
Story of Noah, The, 8
Tailor and the Mouse, The, 152
Three Blind Mice, 133
Tinga Layo, 38
Wise Old Owl, The, 134

Boats and Sailing

Blow Ye Winds, 12
Canoe Song, 33
Come Boating with Me, 27
Down the River, 118
Four in a Boat, 47
Hawaiian Boat Song, 44
Michael, Row the Boat Ashore, 91
Ship A-Sailing, 56

Composed Songs

America, the Beautiful
  (*S. A. Ward*), 20
Clouds (*A. Frackenpohl*), 58
Cuckoo and the Donkey, The
  (*English and German*)
  (*K. F. Zelter*), 150
For the Beauty of the Earth
  (*C. Kocher*), 4
Hallowe'en (*J. Wood*), 46
I Can't Do That Sum
  (*V. Herbert*), 154
Jig Along Home (*W. Guthrie*), 158
Little Jesus Came to Town, The
  (*B. J. Coleman*), 77
Little Sandman, The
  (*J. Brahms*), 92
Little Song of Life, A
  (*W. S. Haynie*), 18
Magic Garden, The
  (*D. Jenni*), 140
O Little Town of Bethlehem
  (*L. H. Redner*), 81
Skater's Waltz
  (*E. Waldteufel*), 110
Some Folks Do (*S. Foster*), 16
Star-Spangled Banner, The
  (*Unknown*), 98
Story of Noah, The
  (*J. J. Niles*), 8
There Are Many Flags in Many
  Lands (*Unknown*), 2
Vesper Hymn (*D. Bortniansky*), 90

Cowboy Songs

Cowboy's Gettin'-Up Holler, 95
Home on the Range, 102
Night Herding Song, 94

Dances and Singing Games

Ali, Ali (Dance the Hora), 107
Brother, Come and Dance
  with Me, 122
Chebogah, 120
Four in a Boat, 47
Hawaiian Boat Song, 44
Needle's Eye, The, 42
Sandy Land, 32
Turn the Glasses Over, 30

Folk Songs from Other Countries

Argentina

My Farm (*English and
  Spanish*), 40

Austria

Austrian Counting Song, 54

Canada

Alouette (*French*), 10
Land of the Silver Birch, 35
'Twas in the Moon of
  Wintertime, 84

Costa Rica

Nonsense Song, 11

Czechoslovakia

Come Tend the Geese, 115

Denmark

Christmas Is Here, 79
Harvest Song, 62

England

Ah, Poor Bird, 69
I Saw Three Ships, 80
Oh, Dear! What Can the
  Matter Be? 112
Ship A-Sailing, 56
Tailor and the Mouse,
  The, 152
This Is My Father's World, 64
We're All Together Again, 15

France

Are You Sleeping? (*French
  and English*), 132
Bring a Torch, Jeannette,
  Isabella, 78
Cloche, La (*French*), 36
Sur le Pont d'Avignon
  (*French*), 23

Germany

Awake and Sing, 60
Brother, Come and Dance
  with Me, 122
Coming of Spring, 147
Juchheidi, Juchheida, 28
Little Man in the Wood, 123
Susy, Little Susy, 121
Weiss sind alle meine
  Kleider (*German*), 101

Holland

Child Was Born upon
  This Earth, A, 82
Once More the Winter's
  Left Us, 160
Sarasponda, 97

162

Alphabetical Index of Music and Poetry

163